Via Dolorosa

Christ's Path *to the* Cross

Dr. Trina Boice

CFI
An imprint of Cedar Fort, Inc.
Springville, Utah

Paperback ISBN 13: 978-1-4621-4956-8
eBook ISBN 13: 978-1-4621-4957-5

Published by CFI, an imprint of Cedar Fort, Inc.
2373 W. 700 S., Suite 100, Springville, UT 84663
Distributed by Cedar Fort, Inc., www.cedarfort.com

Library of Congress Cataloging Number: 2025932364

Cover design by Shawnda Craig

Printed in the United States of America

10 9 8 7 6 5 4 3 2 1

Printed on acid-free paper

Praise for *Via Dolorosa*

Exploring the history and sacred significance of the traditional Via Dolorosa invites us to walk with Christ during His final hours, gaining a deeper appreciation for His infinite sacrifice. Learning about the route's architecture, archaeology, and spiritual heritage enriches our understanding of the Savior's Atonement and Resurrection.

—Dr. John Hilton III, author of *Considering the Cross: How Calvary Connects Us with Christ* and *Please Pass the Scriptures*

Dr. Boice has done it again! Each one of her books is filled with great insights and excellent writing. She includes beautiful images that help the reader visualize and better understand the sacred Via Dolorosa. Thank you again for another precious book.

—Dr. Tracey Long, author of *Ancestry* and *Mommy the Builder*

What a faith-promoting experience to walk the path where Jesus walked. Jerusalem comes alive with images and details and history in this book. This was inspiring.

—Julie Spencer, author of *First Prince of Israel*

I absolutely loved this book. What a treasure. It's perfect as a guidebook for people who travel to Jerusalem, but just as inspirational for those who want to enjoy it from their couch at home! Dr. Boice blends history, culture, scriptures, and personal stories that teach us profound, new insights about the Savior.

—Marci Tanner

Dr. Boice describes the Via Dolorosa as more than just historic steps. The path of Jesus's suffering paves the progress toward his atoning sacrifice. The author applies spiritual meaning when Jesus fulfilled prophecy and paved the way for our resurrection and eternal life. Terrific book.

—Dr. Tera Duncan

DEDICATION

Going to Israel had been a lifelong dream of mine, so when I finally went there for the first time, I was a blubbering mess the entire time! I absolutely loved every minute of it, and I felt it deeply. This book is lovingly dedicated to some wonderful friends who helped make the trip possible and who joined me on my very special and sacred life-changing adventure. I can't wait to return and experience even more amazing locations! As the faithful Jews say, "Next year in Jerusalem!"

John Hilton III
Tom Boice
Larry and Tracey Long
Marlon and Shiobhan Sheridan
Brad and Kathy Peterson

CONTENTS

CHAPTER 1

What Is the Via Dolorosa?

In April 2023, the Prophet and President of The Church of Jesus Christ of Latter-day Saints proclaimed that Easter Sunday is "the most important religious observance for followers of Jesus Christ" and the Atonement and Resurrection of Jesus Christ is "the most important and transcendent event ever recorded on earth."[1] The First Presidency, led by President Nelson, invited everyone to reflect more on the infinite Atonement of Jesus Christ during Easter. A Christ-centered observance of Easter is much more meaningful and appropriate than one filled with chocolate rabbits and brightly colored eggs.

One way to reflect more on the Atonement is to learn about the Via Dolorosa, which is believed to be the route where Jesus was forced by the Roman soldiers to carry the cross from His condemnation to crucifixion. While the Via Dolorosa is an extremely popular tradition and pilgrimage for Christians around the world, few members of The Church of Jesus Christ of Latter-day Saints even know about it. I'm excited to introduce this fascinating tradition with you and pray that it

will enrich your Easter activities each spring, as well as your scripture study efforts all year long.

The New Testament events honored in the Via Dolorosa in Jerusalem, Israel, tell the greatest story ever told. This book has been lovingly designed to give you a taste of this amazing "Way of the Cross" path in Jerusalem that can give you and your family ideas to better focus on the Savior.

Studying the rich history, inspirational stories, intriguing pictures, and spiritual insights just might become your new favorite tradition at Easter time as you read and learn about the last few hours of the Savior's life, the path that made it possible for us to have eternal life.

This book describes the fourteen stations along the Via Dolorosa route in Jerusalem. After I discuss each station, I'll include the biblical references so you can read them and contemplate what they mean to you. Pondering is powerful.

Even more powerful is taking action. At the end of each chapter, I'll share ideas of how you and your family can apply the principles you studied to become more Christlike. We can study the life of Christ and even walk where He walked, but if we're not developing His qualities and attributes, we're missing the whole point!

You can use this as a guidebook when you visit the Old City in Jerusalem, but if you can't go there, it is my hope is that you will study the many symbols and truths in this book to strengthen your own testimony that Jesus is the Christ!

Daniel Rona, a popular Latter-day Saint tour guide in Israel, stated, "The key to recognizing the Messiah and the true meaning of His life, and those who testified of Him, is the Spirit."[2] As you read through the pages in this book, listen closely to the Spirit. Write down questions you want inspiration about. The Holy Ghost will teach you what you need to know, regardless of my words.

The Joseph Smith Translation of Timothy 3:16–17 counsels, "And all scripture given by inspiration of God is profitable for doctrine, for reproof, for correction, for instruction in righteousness: that the man of God may be perfect, thoroughly furnished unto all good works." To summarize, studying the scriptures will do at least four things for us:

1. Teach us truth (doctrine).
2. Point out what we need to change (reproof).
3. Put us back on course (correction).
4. Keep us there (instruction in righteousness).

It warms my heart that millions of Christians around the world are focused on the Savior's atoning sacrifice. Millions of Christians have made pilgrimages to the Via Dolorosa in memory of that sacrifice. We normally associate Easter with Christ's sacrifice for us, but the world celebrates Christmas joyously because of the Atonement.

President Hugh B. Brown stated, "We believe that the greatest story ever told in all the annals of history is the story of the atonement of Christ. The record of his resurrection and ascension, without which the atonement would not have been complete, is the climax to that story; and now over 2000 years after the event, it is still central and pivotal in all true Christian thought."[3]

The Via Dolorosa

Via Dolorosa is not the name of a street. It's believed to be the route Jesus was forced to walk by the Roman soldiers while He carried the cross from His condemnation to crucifixion. It's two thousand feet long, beginning at the Lions' Gate in the Old City of Jerusalem and ending at the Church of the Holy Sepulchre, about a fifteen-minute walk from Gethsemane in the Christian Quarter. In Latin,

Via Dolorosa means "Way of Suffering"; Spanish translates it as the "Painful Path." Other translations describe it as the"Road of Sorrow," "Way of Grief," or "The Way of the Cross."

The Via Dolorosa includes fourteen stations, each representing an event that happened to Jesus on His way to the cross. During the Byzantine era, Christian pilgrims participated in a "Holy Thursday" procession that began at the Mount of Olives, stopped in Gethsemane, and then continued to the Church of the Holy Sepulchre, the site that the mother of Constantine declared as the true site of Jesus's crucifixion and burial. During the eighth century, more locations were added to the route. When the Catholics of Jerusalem split the city into two arguing factions during the Middle Ages (east vs. west), each side declared sacred spots were in their area of the city that they had control over.

It wasn't until the fourteenth century that Pope Clement VI finally put the Franciscan friars in charge of the shrines and pilgrims. They led tours in the reverse order of today's tours. In 1517, they changed the route to go in chronological order of Jesus's Passion. Later, new Christian traditions emerged, and pilgrimages to the Holy Land became even more popular in Europe. For centuries, visitors argued about the authenticity of the various stations. Only seven of the fourteen stations are biblically based; the remaining stations were born out of stories passed down through the ages, becoming Christian tradition.

As more archeologists studied the highlighted areas in the nineteenth and twentieth centuries, the route we know today became clearer and more official. To this day, we can still see Roman pavement along certain areas of the Via Dolorosa route that confirms they were streets during Christ's life. The route has changed several times, but the devotion to Jesus Christ's last hours and the price He paid to redeem mankind from physical and spiritual death has remained. Walking the Via Dolorosa path today is a bittersweet experience for faithful followers of the Savior.

If you are lucky enough to be in Jerusalem on a Friday, you'll get to watch and participate in a Franciscan friar's procession. The friars have been the custodians of the Via Dolorosa since the thirteenth century, and they still carry on this tradition with touching devotion.

They begin at station 1 around 4:00 p.m. (3:00 in the winter) and stop at each of the fourteen stations. They take turns reading scriptures, offering prayers, singing and chanting, and meditating in silence. You can watch videos of their devout procession on YouTube. You can also see nuns pushing pilgrims in wheelchairs and hear groups singing hymns along the way. Re-enactments are often performed with props and period clothing. Escorts of the procession, called Kawas, wear Ottoman uniforms of red fez, gold-embroidered waistcoats, and baggy blue trousers. They bang silver-topped staves (staffs) on the ground to signify their authority.

Some tourist groups on pilgrimage wake up at the crack of dawn so they can visit all the stations before the crowds emerge. While that sounds like a good idea, it prevents them from seeing inside all the amazing churches on those sites and causes them to miss out on much of the rich experience. Most of the churches and shops don't open until 8:00 or 9:00 a.m.

The Fourteen Stations of the Via Dolorosa

The original Via Dolorosa route became popular during the Crusades. Centuries later, because so many non-Catholic Christians were hesitant about the biblical authenticity of the Via Dolorosa, Pope John Paul II came up with the Scriptural Way of the Cross in 1991 to back up the various stations with more scriptural evidence. It includes a set of lovely prayers to go with the scriptures. His list includes nine stations:

1. Pilate condemns Jesus.
2. Jesus accepts the cross.
3. Simon helps Jesus carry the cross.
4. Jesus speaks to women.
5. Jesus is stripped of His garments.
6. Jesus is nailed to the cross.
7. Jesus cares for His mother.
8. Jesus dies on the cross.
9. Jesus is resurrected.

Those stations are taken directly from the New Testament, while all the new ones were born out of Christian tradition. The path of fourteen Stations of the Cross was finalized in the eighteenth century. Today, you can see a big metal map at station 2 that shows the stations along a path from beginning to end. It's written in multiple languages, including English. Nine of the official stations are along the narrow streets in Old Jerusalem, with the last five stations inside the Church of the Holy Sepulchre.

Today, the fourteen stations of Via Dolorosa include these fourteen events:

1. Jesus is condemned to death by crucifixion by Pontius Pilate.
2. Jesus is scourged, given the crown of the thorns, and begins to carry the cross.

3. Jesus falls under the weight of the cross for the first time.
4. Jesus encounters his mother, Mary, along the way.
5. Simon of Cyrene is told by the Roman soldiers to help Jesus carry the cross.
6. A woman named Veronica wipes the sweat and blood from Jesus's face.
7. Jesus falls a second time.
8. Jesus speaks to the women of Jerusalem who are weeping for Him.
9. Jesus falls a third time.
10. Jesus is stripped of His clothes at Golgotha.
11. Jesus is nailed to the cross.
12. Jesus dies on the cross.
13. Jesus's body is removed from the cross.
14. Jesus's body is placed in the tomb.

Station numbers are posted in Roman numerals on a bronze disc marking each station along the Via Dolorosa route to let you know which station you are at. Sometimes, the station number is carved into the stone wall itself. Next to the marker is a small sculpture on the wall that illustrates what happened. Some stations have a small church to commemorate the location, while others display the markers and a sign to identify the site. Despite all of the markers, it's still very easy to get lost because there are so many small passageways that wind like a labyrinth through Old Jerusalem.

You can get a complimentary map of the Via Dolorosa by visiting the Christian Information Center on Omar Ibn el-Khattab Square by Jaffa Gate, as well as in some of the shops along the route. Finding each station along the Via Dolorosa is like a spiritual scavenger hunt. There are many hidden gems along the way, making it easy to get distracted.

It feels odd to walk the path as a spiritual pilgrimage to commemorate the most significant event in human history, all while walking past vendors who are trying to sell their wares to tourists, seeing political propaganda on posters, or hearing angry protesters rant in different languages. Seeing people bow and kneel before each station's spot is humbling and awe-inspiring. It's truly overwhelming to see the faith in others' tear-filled eyes.

Everywhere you go, you will see other individuals and groups from around the world with the same desire of their hearts as yours: to worship and show gratitude for Jesus Christ's atoning sacrifice. Many groups sing touching hymns about the Savior in all languages. It is heartwarming to hear their testimonies sung in different languages; you can tell they are singing hymns they loved and that their souls are worshipping through the music.

Sometimes, the groups recite scriptures at each station. Other times, they walk in silence. It's an honor to walk this route with others who love Jesus as much as we do.

Via Dolorosa is about two thousand feet long (just over a kilometer or half a mile). It's a winding path through the streets of Old Jerusalem and can be done in about two hours, depending on how long you spend at each station. It could have taken between two to four hours for Christ to walk this distance while carrying the cross.

Because there is a Muslim quarter in Old Jerusalem, you will often hear the daily call to prayer on loudspeakers. Jerusalem is the most sacred real estate in the world as the convergence site of three religions: Christianity, Islam, and Judaism. The Old City is constantly under construction with new excavations, scaffolding, tools, and busy workers.

The Via Dolorosa is a vivid tapestry of history, religion, and symbolism, inviting individuals of diverse faiths to embark on a spiritual journey. It is a place where the past meets the present and believers can

connect with their faith and the profound sacrifices made by Jesus. As visitors walk the Via Dolorosa, they become part of an ancient narrative, experiencing the weight of history and the power of devotion.

I truly hope everyone is able to visit Jerusalem one day because it is a magnificent and life-changing experience. That being said, I realize not everyone will be able to do so, especially in today's dangerous political climate. Regardless of whether you are able to travel, we can all learn more about Jesus Christ and express our gratitude for all that He endured for us. President Thomas S. Monson stated:

> We need not visit the Holy Land to feel Him close to us. We need not walk by the shores of Galilee or among the Judean hills to walk where Jesus walked. In a very real sense, all can walk where Jesus walked when, with His words on our lips, His spirt in our hearts, and His teachings in our lives, we journey through mortality.[4]

President Monson also pointed out that Jesus walked the path of pain, disappointment, and temptation.[5] We all experience those things in our life too. But He also walked the path of obedience, service, and prayer. We can do those things too. Each day, we choose whom to follow: Jesus or the world.

Elder Bruce R. McConkie admonished, "In the final analysis, our purpose in learning of our Lord is to gain that knowledge, insight, and desire which will cause us to become like Him."[6]

As awe-inspiring and faith promoting it is to walk *where* Jesus walked, it is more important that we walk *as* Jesus walked.

The Roman Catholic Church

The Roman Catholic Church plays a large role in the history, identification, and construction of many of the sites in Jerusalem on the Via Dolorosa. Inside Catholic cathedrals all over the world, and often in small parish churches, paintings and sculptures around the walls of the nave (the main area) depict the fourteen stations of the cross, or the "Passion" of the Christ. These images are a devotional tool for Catholics, aiding them in meditating on the suffering and sacrifice of Jesus.

Catholics honor the Via Dolorosa through a variety of practices and rituals, particularly during Lent and Holy Week. Here are some of the main ways their practices could be modified for Latter-day Saint families:

1. **Stations of the Cross:** This is a devotional practice where Catholics meditate on the fourteen stations of Jesus's journey to Golgotha. This can take place in a church or outdoors, often following a series of images or sculptures depicting each station. The practice involves prayer and reflection at each station, often accompanied by readings and hymns.
2. **Pilgrimage to Jerusalem:** Some Catholics make a pilgrimage to Jerusalem to walk the actual Via Dolorosa. Pilgrims follow the route through the Old City, stopping at each of the fourteen stations. This pilgrimage is a profound spiritual experience, especially during Holy Week.

3. **Good Friday Services:** On Good Friday, the day commemorating Jesus's crucifixion, many Catholic churches hold special services that include the Stations of the Cross. These services often involve a reenactment of Jesus's journey and the veneration of the cross.
4. **Lenten Devotions:** Throughout Lent, the forty-day period leading up to Easter, Catholics may engage in additional practices to honor the Via Dolorosa, such as attending weekly Stations of the Cross services, fasting, and increased prayer and alms giving.
5. **Passion Plays:** In some communities, Passion plays are performed during Holy Week, dramatizing the events of Jesus's Passion, including His journey along Via Dolorosa. These plays are a way for the community to engage deeply with the story of Jesus's suffering and death.
6. **Personal Meditation and Prayer:** Catholics also honor the Via Dolorosa in their personal prayer, reflecting on the Stations of the Cross and Jesus's sacrifice as a part of their daily or weekly devotions.

The teachings of the Catholic Church focus on the cross and the Atonement. In 1965, the Vatican Council issued the following statement: "What happened in [Jesus's] passion cannot be charged against all the Jews, without distinction, then alive, without distinction, nor against the Jews of today. . . . As the Church has always held and holds now, Christ underwent His passion and death freely, because of the sins of men and out of infinite love, in order that all may reach salvation. It is, therefore, the burden of the Church's preaching to proclaim the cross of Christ as the sign of God's all-embracing love and as the fountain from which every grace flows."[7]

Elder Neal A. Maxwell stated:

> We will end up either choosing Christ's manner of living or His manner of suffering! It is either "suffer even as I" (D&C 19:16–17), or overcome "even as [He] . . . overcame" (Rev. 3:21). His beckoning command is to become "even as I am" (3 Ne. 7:27). The spiritually settled accept that invitation, and "through the atonement of Christ," they *become* and *overcome*!" (Mosiah 3:18, 19).[8] (Original maintained)

The Via Dolorosa is all about the Atonement. This book is all about the Atonement. Easter is all about the Atonement. Our lives should focus on the Atonement. We have been saved!

Bring the Stations to Life

To design a week of true worship before Easter, consider this daily plan with your family.

- **Anointing Saturday**: Mary anoints Jesus with special oil (Luke 7:37–38, 44–46). How do we "anoint" others in word and deed? Choose a way you could serve someone else.
- **Day of Popularity Sunday**: Jesus enters Jerusalem in triumph (Luke 19:35–38). How do we vocally and visually show that we are Christians to the world? Wear a shirt from the popular TV show *The Chosen,* or wear another item of clothing or jewelry that expresses your faith in Christ.
- **Day of Authority Monday**: Christ curses the barren fig tree and cleanses the temple (Luke 19:45–46). What do we need to do to cleanse our own lives? Clean your home and prepare your Sunday clothes and shoes for next week.
- **Day of Conflict Tuesday**: Jesus teaches in the temple and on the Mount of Olives (Matthew 21 & 25). Ask each member of your family, "What think ye of Christ?" Watch the Christian movie *What Think Ye of Christ?*
- **Day of Rest Wednesday**: Jesus spent time with His friends at Bethany. Whom do you choose to spend time with to uplift your soul? Invite friends over for dinner or an uplifting game night. Think of another family or individual you could fellowship.

- **Day of Fellowship Thursday**: Jesus partakes of the Last Supper with His Apostles. When we partake of the sacrament, do we think of Christ? Read the sacrament prayer together as a family and discuss how you could worship more sincerely during sacrament meeting.
- **Day of Suffering Friday**. At sunrise, Jesus is officially condemned, begins the Via Dolorosa, and dies. Review each of the fourteen stations of Via Dolorosa in this book.
- **Day of Silence Saturday**. Guards are placed at the tomb. Begin a social media fast.
- **Resurrection Sunday**. Jesus triumphs and defeats physical and spiritual death (Mark 16:6). Attend Easter service at church to celebrate the Resurrection. Even better, invite non-member friends to join you.

CHAPTER 2

The City of Jerusalem

Jerusalem is a true marvel. There is no place on Earth quite like it. A palpable electricity fills the air where three major religions merge together in exuberant and infectious worship, filling the streets with miracles and testimonies. I hope you will feel that special spirit in the pages of this book as well. The place is holy, but what Jesus did there is what's truly holy.

Because visiting Israel has become increasingly dangerous, this book can serve as a safer alternative to experiencing the Via Dolorosa. If you do want to visit Israel, many tour groups are still taking visitors. Always check with your country's state department for the latest travel advisories about safety. And check my website, www.TrinaBoice.com, to learn about the next tour I'm leading in Israel. I'd love for you to join me!

Use the ideas in this book to apply the principles you learn in your daily walk with Christ. Research and study in no way replace the proper application of what we learn to our lives. It is one thing to know the gospel; it is quite another to know it is true. And knowing it is true and living it is an entirely different matter. Use this book as a workbook to help you detail plans on how to be more like Christ. We are all on our own path and journey to follow in the footsteps of the Savior.

The city of Jerusalem is a "tell," which means "mound" or "hill" in Hebrew and Arabic. In the Bible, people talk about going "up" to Jerusalem, even if they were traveling south, simply because Jerusalem is an elevated city, both physically and spiritually.

Jerusalem was built from layers of many civilizations over time. It is a symbol of many important principles, as it has been built, destroyed, and rebuilt many times:

- Faith
- Conflict and reconciliation toward peace
- The Kingdom of God
- Sacrifice
- Redemption
- Unity and diversity

Jerusalem embodies not only the spiritual aspirations of many but also the struggle and resilience inherent in the human experience, making it a symbol of us—humanity's shared spiritual journey, longing for meaning, and the pursuit of a better world. Jesus "set His face to go to Jerusalem" (Luke 9:51) and knew that His mortal ministry must end in this very symbolic city (Matthew 16:21).

History of Jerusalem in a Nutshell

To better understand the significance of Jerusalem, allow me to give you a very brief summary of its history. According to archeologists, the first settlement in the Jerusalem area dates back to around 3000 BC during the Bronze Age. Jerusalem first appeared in the Bible in Genesis 14:18 as Salem, ruled by Melchizedek, the priest-king. Fast forward to King David, who built Jerusalem as the capital of his Israelite kingdom sometime between 1003 and 997 BC. It became the religious center of Judaism and is still considered by some to be the true homeland of the Jews. Solomon's temple was constructed on what is now known as the Temple Mount. It housed the ark of the covenant, an ornate golden box that contained the original stone tablets upon which God wrote the Ten Commandments and gave to Moses. Some claim the ark of the covenant is hidden somewhere in Jerusalem, while others believe the Pope has it in the Vatican. There is no evidence of its current whereabouts, unless you believe the Indiana Jones movie *The Raiders of the Lost Ark,* which revealed it's in a crate in a giant warehouse somewhere in Washington, DC. (Wink!)

After its glory days during the First Temple, the holy city experienced multiple invasions and destruction over the centuries. The Babylonians destroyed Solomon's temple around 586 BC, carrying off many of the inhabitants to Babylon. The city was rebuilt fifty years later, and the Second Temple was rebuilt. Jerusalem came under Greek rule for a time and was later destroyed by the Romans in AD 70. The Jews today have longed to rebuild their temple in God's city and continue to worship at the last remnants of what they believe to be that temple wall called the Western Wall. Jerusalem is profoundly sacred to our Jewish brothers and sisters.

Because Jesus died in Jerusalem, the city has also become the most sacred spot on Earth for Christians, as evidenced by the Via Dolorosa, the journey millions of religious pilgrims make every year. Muslims tell the story about how their prophet Muhammad, in AD 621, ascended to the heavens from the Temple Mount in Jerusalem, securing the holy city as their third most revered location in all of Islam. They conquered Jerusalem in 637 and claim it as their sacred city.

The famous Crusaders led by the King of England conquered Jerusalem in 1099 as their inspired quest to return the Holy Land and its sacred sites to the Christians. The land was managed under British control all the way up until 1948. After World War II, the British authorities handed the Old City over to the Palestinian State; however, after the Six-day War in 1968, the eastern part of the city where the main religious sites are located was annexed by Israel. Today, ownership of Jerusalem is still debated in heated arguments and bullets.

This book is not designed to showcase *all* the amazing sites within the walls of the Old City in Jerusalem; there are simply too many fascinating locations to talk about. The focus of this book is to introduce you to the Via Dolorosa, which highlights where the Savior walked from condemnation to crucifixion in the last hours of His life.

The Four Quarters of Jerusalem

Today, the Old City is a walled area a little more than a third of a square mile that includes religious and historical significance for Christianity, Judaism, and Islam. The Old City is divided into four quarters: Muslim, Jewish, Christian, and Armenian. The New City of

Jerusalem refers to modern areas outside the Old City walls, developed primarily in the nineteenth century onward.

The Muslim Quarter is the largest and most populous of the four quarters in the Old City and has tons of shops and fun foods to try. The energetic bazaar (marketplace) is called a souk, stretching block after block in the area. The Ottoman-era buildings feature arched doorways and intricate tiles. Its gem is the Temple Mount with the Al-Aqsa Mosque and the Dome of the Rock, both heavily guarded by armed soldiers. You will find quite a few access points to the Temple Mount platform for Muslims but only one for Christians and Jews: the Mughrabi Gate (Moroccan Gate).

In case you're wondering how the guards at all of those Muslims gates know if you're Muslim or not, they know! Access through those gates is managed by the Islamic Waqf who run through certain procedures when you try to get in. They first consider your ethnic appearance, language, and clothing. Then, they may ask you questions about Islamic practices or beliefs, testing your knowledge of the Qur'an (Koran), Islamic greetings, or certain prayers. In some cases, visitors might even be asked to show documentation. If you're not Muslim, just go to the Mughrabi Gate.

As a Christian, it is a bit nerve-wracking to walk through the correct entrance. Soldiers with machine guns stand at the gate to run your purse or backpack through an X-ray machine with an additional visual check. No scriptures are allowed except the Qur'an. A week before my group was scheduled to fly to Israel, a violent skirmish broke out between Jews and Muslims at the Mughrabi Gate, resulting in gunfire. Frightened for our safety, I asked our tour company if we should cancel our trip. "Nah, this happens all the time!" he assured me. Somehow, I didn't feel very assured!

Things calmed down a bit, and we flew to Israel on schedule. Once there, we all felt perfectly safe and cared for.

The Via Dolorosa route begins within the grounds of the Muslim Quarter at the Antonia Fortress.

The Jewish Quarter contains the Cardo Maximus, a main thoroughfare that ran through the center of the city of Jerusalem in Emperor Hadrian's day in AD 135. Back then, it was flanked by two rows of Roman columns. You can still see a few remaining

columns in a section of the city. It was the main commercial area in Jerusalem for nearly five hundred years, dating from the second to third centuries AD.

Hadrian (Publius Aelius Hadrianus) was a Roman emperor who ruled from AD 117 to 138. He renamed Jerusalem Aelia Capitolina and renamed Israel Palestine in an attempt to erase any connection the Jews had to their declared homeland. He tried to recreate Jerusalem into a city with the Cardo Maximus running the full length of the city. At the site of Golgotha, which early Christians venerated, Hadrian built a temple to honor Jupiter (Jove) and Aphrodite (Venus), two gods in Roman mythology. He designed the Cardo to run right next to the temple to make it easy for everyone to worship them. Christians and Jews were furious.

Later, when Roman Emperor Constantine converted to Christianity, he tore down the Roman temple and built the Christian Church of the Holy Sepulchre in its first iteration. The Crusaders changed part of the church centuries later. This is a perfect example of a site that has been built and rebuilt, layer upon layer, in Jerusalem. You can still see part of Hadrian's temple wall in the lower level of the Church of the Holy Sepulchre. Five of the stations of the Via Dolorosa are inside that church, so I'll discuss it in greater detail in future chapters.

The most sacred spot in the Jewish Quarter is the famous Western Wall, also called the Wailing Wall. Jews believe it is the last remaining wall of the Second Temple which was destroyed by the Romans. Some archeologists insist it is not. In Jewish tradition, the Western Wall of the Temple Mount is significant because it marks the Foundation Stone, the place where some believe Adam was created at the beginning of the world. Jews believe that the Divine Presence (God) never left the Western Wall after the Second Temple was destroyed, so they go to the wall to pray every day. Every Jewish synagogue in the world is designed to face east toward the city of Jerusalem.

One of the most incredible experiences I had in Jerusalem was celebrating with the Jews on their Shabbat (sabbath) at the Western Wall. The air was filled with an excitement and sense of joy that I've never seen practiced by any other religion. You can read about my experience in chapter 17. I get teary-eyed just thinking about it!

The rest of the Jewish Quarter is relatively quiet and much more residential than anywhere else in the Old City.

The Christian Quarter gets the most international tourists from around the world because it features so many sacred sites in Christianity. There is much to see and learn about where Jesus spent His time here. Religious pilgrims come from across the globe to walk in His footsteps and worship in their unique ways. If you look at the route of the Via Dolorosa, you will see it dotted with countless churches, monasteries, and memorials to Jesus Christ even as it winds through Muslim territory.

Most of the Christian churches in Jerusalem, as well as their traditions, are unbelievably old. All over Israel, you will see Christians traveling in groups at the biblical sites to pay homage to the role they played in the life of Jesus. Sometimes, they wear matching hats or scarves so they don't get lost from each other in the crowds.

While my group sang our beloved hymns in English, we could hear nearby groups singing theirs in other languages. The melodies weren't familiar to us, but their love for the Lord was. We all sang the songs of redeeming love. It was so sweet and magical.

If you're reading a chapter of this book each day with your family to prepare for Easter, be sure to sing a hymn together too. Music is so powerful and speaks to the soul in such a unique way.

Many people are surprised to hear there is an Armenian Quarter in Jerusalem. It is much smaller and in poor shape due to building restrictions. It is said that Armenia was the first country to adopt Christianity in the fourth century as its official religion. You'll learn more about their contributions to Christianity when we get to the end of the Via Dolorosa route at station 14.

The Armenian Quarter in the Old City houses many Armenian monks, the Cathedral of St. James, and the Monastery of St. Mark. Its biggest claim to fame is that many Christian denominations believe The Last Supper took place in an upstairs room of one of its buildings. Other scholars place the traditional site outside the Old City walls near the Zion Gate in the Cenacle. We don't know for sure what the true site was.

Within the walls of the Old City, you may see golf carts and other tiny vehicles that are generally used to remove trash and bring in supplies during certain hours. Only a few cars are allowed entrance if they have special permits for things like emergency services, maintenance, or authorized residents. No parking is allowed, so visitors will definitely need to park outside the walls. The city itself is extremely walkable. The narrow streets are charming and create a truly immersive experience in this noisy, vibrant city.

The Twelve Gates of Jerusalem

An interesting note is that there were twelve gates into the Old City of Jerusalem, representing the twelve tribes of Israel. The number twelve in Bible numerology represents divine government or that God rules His people. Notice that Jesus had twelve apostles. Jesus's first recorded words were when He was twelve. When Jesus performed the miracle of the feeding of the five thousand, twelve baskets were filled with leftovers (Matthew 14:13–21; Mark 6:31–44; Luke 9:12–17; John 6:1–14).

Elijah built an altar of twelve stones (1 Kings 18). God required that twelve unleavened bread cakes be placed in the temple each week (Leviticus 24). Those are just a few examples in the Bible of how God is trying to teach us about His divine governance and order. God loves symbols because they transcend language. He gives us breadcrumbs to follow if we're paying attention.

Historically, the gates in the north wall were named for Reuben, Judah, and Levi. On each of the gates were written the corresponding names. The gates on the east wall were designated for Joseph, Ben, and Dan. The south wall gates were named for Simeon, Issachar, and Zebulun, and the west wall gates were named for Gad, Asher, and Naphtali (Ezekiel 48:31–34).

The Golden Gate

The gate considered to be the most important one is the Golden Gate, also known as the Gate of Mercy, Beautiful Gate (Acts 3:2–10), and the Eastern Gate. The Bible tells us that when the Messiah comes, He will enter through the eastern gate (Zechariah 14:4, Ezekiel 44:1–2, Ezekiel 46:12, and Matthew 24:27). Both Jews and Christians believe that. In Islam, it is where final judgment will occur and is known as the Gate of Eternal Life and Gate of Repentance. The most important direction for the ancient inhabitants of the Holy Land was east. All directions in the Bible are given as if standing and looking to the east. Have you ever noticed that?

Christians believe that Jesus Christ *did* enter through the east gate, the Golden Gate, on Palm Sunday as His triumphal entry, implying His own messianic status (Matthew 21; Mark 11; John 12). If He were a soldier going to war, He would have ridden a horse, but instead, He followed the tradition of riding a donkey, which is what kings did. King Solomon also rode a donkey as a symbol of peace when he was appointed king (Zechariah 9:9; Isaiah 62:11). Jesus is the King of Kings.

Speaking of Palm Sunday, I visited Jerusalem shortly after Palm Sunday one year and was thrilled to see palm branches still strung up on various buildings. The Assyrians believed that the canopy of the branch represented heaven and the trunk represented earth. At the Jewish Feast of Tabernacles (Sukkot), usually held in October, Jews celebrate God's deliverance of Israel into the promised land. The Jews chant "Hosanna" and wave palm branches.

Ready to have your mind blown? The members of The Church of Jesus Christ of Latter-day Saints did that same Hosanna Shout at

the dedication of the Kirtland Temple on the exact same day in April 1836, the first time in this dispensation. Palm Sunday was again celebrated by the Church in April 2020, the two hundredth anniversary of the First Vision. During general conference, members of the Church all over the world joined the prophet in waving white handkerchiefs while doing the Hosanna shout.

During that same conference, President Nelson announced the Church's new symbol to the world: an image of the living, resurrected Jesus Christ emerging from the tomb three days after His death. He is standing on a solid foundation, illustrating that He is central in all the Church does. Jesus Christ is the chief cornerstone (Ephesians 2:20). President Russell M. Nelson described the logo as a new visual identifier.

If you line up the image of Jesus Christ in that arch on the new symbol, it is an exact match of the dimensions of the Golden Gate arch in Jerusalem. Was the perfect match a coincidence? I don't think so at all. When President Nelson talk introduced the new symbol, he referred to a scripture in the book of Esther 4:16 that used the word "Shushan" (Hebrew), which is another name for the Golden Gate from the Second Temple period in the first century AD. A lot of sacred things happened at that memorable and historic conference, often without members of the Church realizing it. God gives us breadcrumbs!

The Golden Gate faces the Mount of Olives to the east. Coincidence? No! The Bible tells us the Messiah will come to the Mount of Olives, east of Jerusalem (Zechariah 14; Acts 1:9–12; Matthew 24:3). The BYU Jerusalem Center is also located on the Mount of Olives.

In AD 810, the Golden Gate was sealed by the Arabs and then reopened by the Crusaders in 1102.

Saladin, the first Sultan of Egypt and Syria during the Third Crusade, walled it up again in 1187. The Old City was rebuilt, and the exterior portion of the Golden Gate was sealed for the final time in 1541 by the Ottoman Sultan Suleiman. Some say he sealed it to better defend the city, while others contend that he wanted to prevent the fulfillment of the Jewish prophecy of a Messiah. It has been closed for almost five hundred years and is believed to remain sealed until the Messiah comes. In 2019, the interior of the gate was reopened for Muslim worshipers from the Temple Mount; however, the actual gate Golden Gate is still sealed.

Today, there are only eight remaining gates in the Old City in Jerusalem. The most popular gates for tourists to enter the city are Damascus (Muslims) and Jaffa (Christians and Jews). Many of the gates were destroyed during conquests, rebuilt, or modified over the centuries.

Do you want to hear something cool about Jerusalem? If you draw a line through the three main valleys that run through Jerusalem (Kidron, Hinnom, and Tyropoeon) and connect them on the bottom, you get an image that looks like a crown and creates the Hebrew letter "shin." Shin has quite a few meanings, including divine power, peace, penitence, and Day of Atonement. Shin also stands for the name God: Shaddai. Jerusalem truly is the crown city of God.

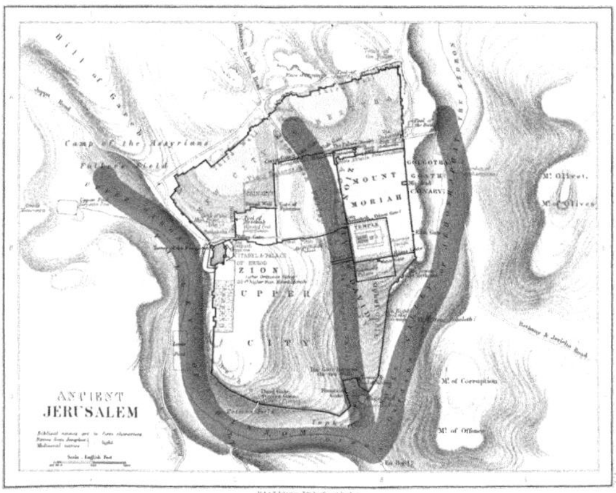

CHAPTER 3

STATION 1
Jesus Is Condemned

Begin by entering the Lions' Gate. To get there, walk about ten minutes on Al-Wad Street and then veer left onto Via Dolorosa Street until you reach the Lions' Gate (St. Stephen's Gate) at the other side of the Old City. Lions' Gate is a popular entrance in the Muslim Quarter because it grants direct access to the Temple Mount. Non-Muslims are not allowed to enter the Temple Mount through that side, however.

If you're traveling with a big tour group, your hotel will most likely be on the other side of Old Jerusalem City, so you can begin by walking through the Damascus Gate in the Muslim Quarter. It is the largest of

the seven open gates and is on the northern side of the city. It will look like an elaborate movie set, but it's the real deal.

The Muslim Quarter is the largest and most populated of the four quarters of the Old City. When I first walked through the Damascus Gate, hundreds of people were pouring out in the opposite direction, and I felt like a salmon swimming upstream. I asked a man what was going on, and he was shocked and offended that I didn't know. He barked at me, "Muslims are invisible in Jerusalem!" and then began a heated argument in Arabic with the man next to him. It was Friday afternoon, so every Muslim in the quarter was closing their shops and heading home after worshipping on Temple Mount.

On Fridays, Muslims worship by attending Jumu'ah (Friday prayer) in their local mosque. Jumu'ah is considered one of the most significant acts of worship in Islam. It is the most holy day to Muslims. Attendance is mandatory for adult men. Women and children are welcome to attend but are not obligated.

To prepare, they perform a full-body purification (ritual washing), often wear special clothing, and apply perfume. Their noon prayer (Dhuhr) takes place after the sun has passed its zenith (midday).

At the mosque, the imam (a religious leader in Islam) delivers a sermon (khutbah) which begins with spiritual messages from the Qur'an and finishes with supplications and advice, usually spoken in Arabic or the local language. Afterward, the imam leads the group in two prayers and then invites participants to make personal prayers.

In only a few hours, hundreds and hundreds of Jews will pour into the city to celebrate their Sabbath (Shabbat) at the Western Wall, observed every Friday night from sunset to Saturday night's sunset. Needless to say, tensions are still very high between Jews and Muslims in Jerusalem, so it was so wonderful to see that they gave space to each other to worship in their own way on the Temple Mount on Fridays.

You will see many interesting things in the Muslim Quarter and want to taste all of the new, interesting foods sold in the street along the way. Do it! Be sure to try the bread called Ka'ak al-quds, long, oblong-shaped bread sticks with a delightfully high crust-to-soft-interior ratio. It's known as Jerusalem Sesame Bread and might remind you of gigantic bagels. The locals pull off a piece and dip it in hyssop or za'atar, a savory Middle Eastern herb blend of oregano, thyme, sesame seeds, and sumac. The flavor is distinctly savory and delicious. Bottles and bags of za'atar are sold in many of the tourist shops in the city.

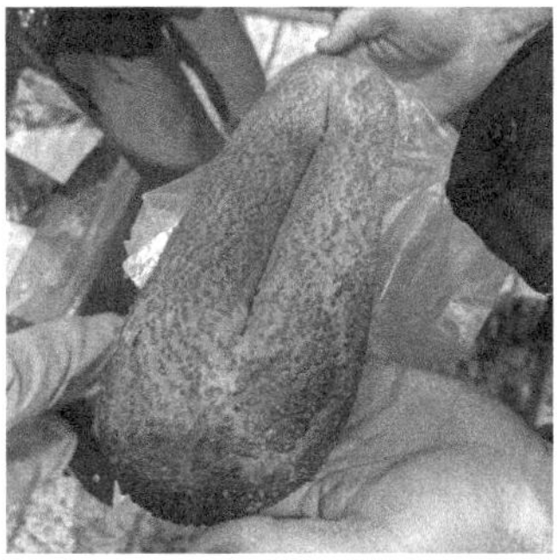

The Praetorium

The New Testament explains that Pontius Pilate condemned Jesus in the Praetorium (Mark 15:16). *Praetorium* is a Latin name for the location where the Roman governor would conduct business and judgments, giving the palace the nickname "hall of judgment" (John 18:28, 33; 19:9–13; Acts 23:35). All four Gospels (Matthew, Mark, Luke, and John) mentioned the Praetorium; however, we don't know exactly where it was. There are three current theories about its most likely location:

1. Herod the Great's palace was known as the Citadel and a place where Roman soldiers would have been. This location dominated the Upper City, just inside the Jaffa Gate. It included

the Tower of David (erected after King David's time during the Early Muslim Period around 24 BC), which still stands as a medieval fortress and popular landmark of Jerusalem.[9]

2. The Palace of the Hasmoneans does not currently exist but would have been located somewhere between Herod's Palace and the temple, which today is in the Jewish Quarter. The palace was built before Herod's time and was used to house the rulers of Judea.
3. The Antonia Fortress was a huge military garrison built by Herod the Great. It was situated north of the temple compound. A few remaining ruins still stand today. Because many believe that location to be the true site of the Praetorium spoken about in the scriptures, that is where the Via Dolorosa begins. Of course, archaeologists are still debating that point.

Station 1 begins where the Herodian Antonia Fortress was said to be located in Roman times. The original fortress has since been destroyed and built over. Many of the buildings here date back to the fourteenth century when they were used as barracks. Station 1 is kind of hidden behind the entrance to what is now the Islamic Al Omariyeh (Umariya) boys' elementary school today. Because it's a private school, groups are no longer allowed inside during school hours.

When I was there, I saw a large sign that announced we were at station 1, but it was unclear where to go. I saw a ramp, and because I am extremely curious, I walked up it. I peeked in an open metal door and found a man who spoke English. He was the groundskeeper and said that we were, indeed, at station 1.

The elementary school is built on the traditional site of the old Antonia Fortress. Archeologists have been able to confirm that area was used for public gatherings and that there was a cemetery on the other side, outside the city

wall, where many people believe Golgotha was located. I'll talk more about the disputed sites of Golgotha after station 14.

The groundskeeper of the school walked us over to an area where we could see an incredible view of the Temple Mount, which is on the other side of the wall that separates it from the old Antonia Fortress. Tradition says that soldiers were placed at the Antonia Fortress to guard the temple.

While this station begins the official Via Dolorosa route, it doesn't fully tell the story of Jesus's condemnation. Prior to meeting with Pontius Pilate on this site, Jesus had been arraigned by the Israelite leaders of the day: Annas (the former high priest), then Caiaphas (the current high priest who was also Annas's son-in-law). Next, Jesus was brought before the Roman leaders: Herod Antipas (the tetrarch of Galilee) and Pontius Pilate (the Roman governor in Judea). This station on the path to the cross commemorates the second time Pontius met with Jesus. We have no record that anyone came to speak up in Jesus's defense. He was utterly alone to walk this path to His destiny.

Some biblical scholars believe Pontius Pilate carried out this "trial" at Herod's Palace, which is near the Tower of David and the Church of the Holy Sepulchre today. Others believe all of this occurred on the southwest side of the wall of the Antonia Fortress. Again, archeologists and biblical scholars are still debating the correct location.

While at the Antonia Fortress site, we walked into an open courtyard made of stones. It is believed to be where Jesus was sentenced by Pontius Pilate. Pilate had asked the crowd what he should do with Jesus. The crowd yelled, "Crucify him!" Then Pilate asked the crowd what crime Jesus had committed, only to be answered with louder cries of "Crucify him!"

Pilate took water and washed his hands of the entire matter, thinking that would absolve him of his own horrific crime. He claimed he was innocent of Jesus's blood and that it would now be the crowd's responsibility. He declared, "I am innocent of this man's blood" (Matthew 27:24). Despite his reluctance, he authorized Jesus's crucifixion, a decision that solidified his historical infamy.

Though we haven't issued the official condemnation that Pilate did, we are all guilty of the pain we caused Jesus, simply by the sins we have committed. No one can wash their hands of that shame because Jesus was the only human to ever live without committing sin. That fact is what makes the Savior's Atonement intimately personal to each of us. He was there to meet the demands of mercy and justice.

Jesus did not defend Himself and willingly allowed everything to unfold as it did because He knew it was to this end He was born: to atone for the sins of mankind (John 18:37).

What Kind of a Man Was Pontius Pilate?

Pontius Pilate was the Roman governor, or prefect, of the province of Judea when Jesus was crucified. Appointed by Emperor Tiberius, Pilate served as the representative of Roman authority in Judea for a ten-year span filled with brutal politics. His primary role was to maintain order in Judea, enforce Roman law, oversee tax collection, and ensure loyalty to the Roman Empire in a region known for its political and religious tensions.

He's a biblical "character" who actually adds to the credibility of scripture because we have archeological evidence that he did exist. In 1961, a team of archeologists were excavating in Caesarea Maritima and found what they called the Pilate Stone, a fractured piece of limestone with an inscription with Pilate's name and a dedication to the spot to the "divine" Tiberius. Scholars believe that site to have been a temple built to honor Tiberius. The age of the stone and engraved dates match what we learn in the New Testament, as Tiberius served as the Roman emperor from AD 14 to 37. Pilate held his post in Judea from AD 26 to 36.

As the governor of the region, Pontius Pilate was a military leader but also a high priest of the Roman religion, which honored Tiberius as a god. The distinctive religion of the monotheistic Jews in Judea was difficult for the polytheistic Romans to understand or agree with. Josephus, the Jewish historian, wrote about massive Jewish protests when Pontius Pilate placed graven images of Tiberius on standards in Jerusalem. He was determined to make a strong statement upon his arrival as the new governor. He most definitely did, and the Jews hated him for it.

The first task of a Roman governor was to preserve peace. He went to Jerusalem three times a year to manage the volatile feast days and remind everyone that Rome was in charge. Ironically, the fact that he brought fresh troops with him each time made riots even more likely. His peacekeeping efforts resulted in the opposite situation.

Each time Pilate asked the crowd what he should do with the King of the Jews and the people answered, "Crucify him!," he was cementing in their minds that there would be "no king other than Caesar" by Roman rule (John 19:15). Pilate's final act of contempt for any Jew who claimed to usurp his and Rome's political power was the sign he placed on the cross of the Christ: "Jesus of Nazareth, the King of the Jews." When the Jews tried to correct Pilate by saying Jesus wasn't their king but had only said He was, Pilate emphatically stated, "What I have written, I have written" (John 19:19–22). In effect, he was condemning and mocking all Jews. But Pilate was wrong. Jesus was not only the King of the Jews but the King of all Kings.

Pilate was considered a brutal, bloodthirsty man, even by his fellow Romans. That's saying quite a bit! His strict rule by Rome's authority to keep the people in order might be what got him the job—either that or no one else wanted the tricky job in Jerusalem. It was likely both. Accepting a position in Judea was not desirable for its known anti-Roman sentiment and resulting political uprisings. The position of serving as prefect would have been connected to both prestige and embarrassment for him.

Pilate is most famously remembered for his role in the trial and crucifixion of Jesus Christ, as recorded in the New Testament Gospels. According to the accounts in Matthew 27, Mark 15, Luke 23, and John 18–19, Pilate presided over Jesus's trial. Although he initially found no fault in Jesus and expressed hesitation about sentencing Him to death, Pilate ultimately yielded to the demands of the Jewish leaders and the crowd, who called for Jesus's crucifixion. Some scholars believe Pontius Pilate's resistance was simply a shrewd act of politics so that he could gain favor in the eyes of the Sanhedrin who would owe him a favor later on. The Sanhedrin was the supreme legislative and judicial body in ancient Israel.

The original crime the Sanhedrin brought against Jesus was blasphemy for claiming to be the Son of God, the greatest crime in Jewish law. When the Roman leadership heard Jesus was being called the King of the Jews, they shifted the charge to treason (Luke 23:1–2), making Him an example to all those who questioned Rome's political authority.

Pilate's governance in Judea was marked by tensions with the Jewish population. Historical sources, including the Jewish historian Josephus and the Roman historian Tacitus, describe Pilate as a ruler who often acted with insensitivity and brutality toward Jewish customs. For instance, Pilate reportedly provoked outrage by bringing Roman military standards bearing the emperor's image into Jerusalem, violating Jewish prohibitions against graven images. The Jews were furious and revolted. Pontius Pilate was ready to slaughter them all but was stunned into inaction when he saw the humble Jews bow down and show their necks, willing to die for their religious values. Josephus tells us that Pilate was actually impressed by their resolve and decided to spare them.

But that wasn't his only confrontation with the Jewish people. Another time, he used funds from the temple treasury to build an aqueduct, further inflaming public resentment. This time, Pilate crushed those who protested.

Pilate's eventual fate is less certain and varies between historical and Christian traditions. According to Josephus and Philo of Alexandria, Pilate was removed from his position and recalled to Rome around AD 36, shortly after Jesus was crucified. Roman leaders were furious when they learned Pilate had slaughtered a group of Samaritans because he thought they were planning a rebellion and revolution. In reality, the Samaritans had been on a hill, searching for artifacts they believed to be from Moses.

Some traditions suggest Pontius Pilate was exiled, while others claim he died by suicide, possibly due to disgrace or political pressures. Early Christian writers offer differing accounts, with some portraying Pilate as penitent and even sympathetic to Jesus, leading to conflicting evaluations of his legacy.

Pontius Pilate remains a complex figure in history and theology. As the Roman official who sentenced Jesus to death, he is a pivotal character in the Passion narrative. His actions and motivations have been debated for centuries, with some viewing him as a weak and indecisive administrator, others as a cruel enforcer of Roman rule, and still others as a reluctant participant in a divine plan. His life and governance offer insight into the challenges of Roman provincial administration and the interplay between imperial authority and local religious traditions in the ancient world.

Pilate is most remembered for his indecision about Jesus. Every day, we have the opportunity to be decisive about who we believe Jesus is.

What Kind of Man Was Barabbas?

Biblical and historical scholars have written volumes about Barabbas and his role in Jesus's condemnation by Pilate. All four Gospels mention him: Matthew 27:16–26, Mark 15:6–15, Luke 23:18–23, and John 18:40. So, what do we really know about him?

During the Passover season, it was customary for the Roman governor to release one prisoner chosen by the crowd. Pilate stood before the crowd and asked them which one should be released: Jesus, the King of the Jews, or Barabbas, a notorious prisoner and robber (John 18:40). Mark 15:7 even describes Barabbas as a rebel and a murderer.

Some scholars have questioned what kind of man Barabbas really was, suggesting he was not a criminal but a protestor. The Greek word for robber is *kleptes,* which is where we get the word *kleptomaniac,* or thief. But the Greek word used to describe Barabbas in an earlier translation was *lestes,* which means bandit or insurrectionist.

Barabbas had been known as a revolutionary that stirred up the crowd in an attempt to defy Roman rule. Only a few days prior to the so-called trial, Jesus had just ridden into Jerusalem on a donkey, being hailed as the King of Kings. Pontius Pilate knew he needed to suppress Jewish uprisings, so neither Barabbas nor Christ was a good option for him. They were both a threat to Pilate's ability to control the Jewish masses.

The crowd immediately yelled for Barabbas's release.

While Barabbas was a real man, he also represented all of us, guilty sinners. Have you ever thought of it like that? *We* are Barabbas. Jesus was crucified for all, the best of us and the worst of us.

According to a 1901 Jewish encyclopedia, the name Barabbas means "son of the father" in Aramaic, which some theologians have pointed out as a symbolic contrast to Jesus, who claimed He is the Son of God. As a known insurrectionist, Barabbas was unable to deliver

his people. As the Son of God and Savior of the world, Jesus *did* deliver His people.

According to early Greek and Syriac manuscripts, Barabbas's full name was Yeshua Barabbas . . . Jesus Barabbas. The encyclopedia entry explains, "Accordingly, the first name was afterward omitted from the many scripts of the Gospels when the name of Jesus had become sacred."[10] Bar means "son of," and Abba means "father."

Elder Rulon S. Wells testified, "No greater work has the Lord God of heaven ever undertaken than to save the souls of his children. It is the grandest, the greatest undertaking that ever has been inaugurated."[11]

Continuing on the Via Dolorosa Route

To get to the next station on the Via Dolorosa, walk across the narrow street. It has a convenient handrail on the right side of the stone wall to provide stability for any wobbly bodies that might need assistance on the uneven stones. It's ironic that this is the same street where Jesus would begin His walk to His brutal crucifixion, where His body would be sacrificed to help us all defeat physical and spiritual death.

Be sure to step inside some of the tourist shops. Inside some of the shops, the walls are made of bedrock. The Palace is the most famous shop you'll pass on this street that has this. Bedrock is significant because it suggests it might have been part of the Antonia Fortress complex. Because the Antonia Fortress walls were next to the Temple Mount, some of the bedrock could possibly have been part of the Temple Mount foundation or walls. (By the way, the owner of The Palace shop offers to show visitors inside station 1, as long as school isn't in session.)

As you walk on this long street, you'll see a sign on your right that merges into a small alley called The Nuns Ascent that says "Lithostrotos." According to the Gospel of John, Jesus was taken to the Lithostrotos, which means "the stone paved area," after His

condemnation trial. The first and second stations both have large stone areas from Jesus's time that could prove this was part of the Praetorium compound. We'll discuss the Lithostrotos more in the next chapter.

Related Scriptures

The Bible, primarily the Gospels, contains several accounts of Jesus being condemned by Pontius Pilate. Here are the key passages:

Matthew 27:11–27

- Jesus stands trial before Pilate, who questions Him about being the King of the Jews.
- Pilate offers to release Jesus or Barabbas, a notorious prisoner.
- The crowd chooses Barabbas and demands Jesus be crucified.
- Pilate symbolically washes his hands, declaring himself innocent of Jesus's blood, and hands Jesus over for crucifixion.

Mark 15:1–16

- Early in the morning, Jesus is brought to Pilate by the chief priests.
- Pilate questions Jesus and is amazed at His silence in response to accusations.
- Pilate offers to release Jesus or Barabbas, and the crowd demands Barabbas.

- Pilate, wanting to satisfy the crowd, orders Jesus to be scourged and crucified.

Luke 23:1–25

- The Jewish leaders accuse Jesus of subverting the nation and claiming to be a king.
- Pilate finds no basis for a charge against Him and sends Him to Herod, who also does not find Him guilty.
- Pilate again declares Jesus innocent, but the crowd insists on His crucifixion.
- Pilate finally gives in to their demand and releases Barabbas instead.

John 18:28–19:8–16

- The Jewish leaders take Jesus to Pilate's headquarters early in the morning.
- Pilate questions Jesus about His kingship and truth.
- Pilate finds no fault in Jesus, but the crowd insists on His crucifixion.
- Pilate tries to release Jesus, but the crowd accuses Pilate of opposing Caesar.
- Pilate ultimately hands Jesus over to be crucified.

Acts 3:13–15

- In a sermon, the Apostle Peter recounts Pilate's role in condemning Jesus despite Pilate's initial inclination to release Him.

Acts 13:27–28

- The Apostle Paul mentions that the leaders in Jerusalem and Pilate condemned Jesus, fulfilling prophecy.

Bring This Station to Life

Download the free Via Dolorosa Way of the Cross app. You'll be able to see maps and photos of each station mentioned in this book. You could even recreate a mini version of the Via Dolorosa in your home, where you'll read the scriptures that accompany each station and learn about the events that occurred there.

Suggested Hymns to Sing as a Family

197: O Savior, Thou Who Wearest a Crown
134: I Believe in Christ
34: O Ye Mountains High

CHAPTER 4

STATION 2
Jesus Takes Up the Cross

Station 2 is across the street from station 1, next to the Ecce Homo arch you will see above your head. Look for the sign that says "II Statio." Ecce Homo commemorates Pontius Pilate washing his hands of Jesus's case and giving his famous "Ecce Homo" speech, which means "Behold, the man!" (John 19:1–3, 13, 16–17). Hadrian built the arch in AD 135 as part of a triple arch gate to a plaza that existed at the time. You can see the other two smaller arches inside the two churches next to it: a Christian chapel and a Muslim mosque. Only in Jerusalem!

With the deliberate choice of his mocking words, Pontius Pilate was making it clear to the crowd that Jesus was not the Son of God, as He claimed, but an ordinary man subject to death like all of us. Of course, Pontius Pilate was wrong.

Many have asked who this Jesus was. He had no servants,

yet he was called Master; no degree, yet called Teacher; no medicines, yet called Healer. He had no army, yet kings feared Him. He won no military battles, yet He conquered the world. He committed no crime, yet they crucified Him. He was buried in a tomb, yet He lives today.

The British writer and apologetic Christian C. S. Lewis explained the "trilemma" that we face when trying to decide who Jesus Christ was and is:

> First, if he claims to be God and yet in fact is not, he has to be a madman or a lunatic.
>
> Second, if he is neither God nor a lunatic, he has to be a liar, deceiving others by his lie.
>
> Third, if he is neither of these, he must be God.
>
> You can only choose one of the three possibilities.
>
> If you do not believe that he is God, you have to consider him a madman.
>
> If you cannot take him for either of the two, you have to take him for a liar.
>
> There is no need for us to prove if Jesus of Nazareth is God or not. All we have to do is find out if He is a lunatic or a liar. If He is neither, He must be the Son of God.[12]

Station 2 is a compound of two Roman Catholic churches within a Franciscan monastery: the Church of Flagellation and the Church of the Condemnation and Imposition of the Cross. Some archeologists contend that these buildings would have been part of the original Antonia Fortress. As you enter the compound, you will see a fantastic bas relief model on the wall of the first century AD of Old Jerusalem. It will help you get a better visual understanding of how locations are situated as you walk the Way of the Cross.

The Church of Flagellation

It is believed that the Church of Flagellation was erected on the site in the twelfth century. It was subsequently used as a dump for waste, a stable, and a weaver's shop. The church was restored between 1927 and 1929 to commemorate where Jesus was flogged after condemnation.

It was built by a famous Italian architect Antonio Barluzzi, who also designed other lovely buildings in the Holy Land.

The three beautiful stained glass window panels inside the Church of Flagellation are the work of L. Picchiarini and feature images of Pontius Pilate washing his hands, Jesus Christ being flogged, and Barrabas being released. On the ceiling is a fantastic mosaic called the *Crown of Thorns Pierced by Stars,* which represents the crown of thorns that was put on the Savior's head. On the tips of the thorns, you can see small drops of blood. In the Holy Land, a plant called"Zizi-phus spina-christi is the traditional candidate for the origin of those thorny branches. Its flexibility would have allowed the Roman soldiers to bend it into a woven crown of thorns. Today, that plant is known as the Christ-thorn plant. In the Christian view, that crown of thorns was an important antecedent to Jesus's ultimate crown of glory.

Matthew 27:28 tells us that the Roman soldiers also put a scarlet robe on Jesus to finish off His derisive royal outfit. The color scarlet was associated with the guilt of a sinner (Isaiah 1:18) and was used to describe things that were sinful or evil. In contrast, the darker color of scarlet, purple, represented royalty (Mark 15:17).

The small chapel feels relatively bright, respectful, and peaceful, which is surprising when considering what happened on this site. Catholics call this the second Sorrowful Mystery of the Rosary and recognize it as the sixth station of Pope John Paul II's scripture-based Via Dolorosa route mentioned in chapter 1.

As you walk at this site, notice the floor made of large paving stones. Some of the Roman flagstones show grooves and games cut into the stone, something you will see on some of the paved streets in the Old City. People played a popular dice game called The King's Game on these stones. You'll also see these markings on the pavement in the lower levels at the Sisters of Zion Convent (The Church of the Sisters of Notre Dame De Sion).

The Flagellation Museum displays quite a few artifacts from several sites in the Holy Land:

Nazareth, Capernaum, and the Mount of Olives. It's open every day except Sunday and Monday.

After visiting both chapels, you'll exit the Franciscan compound and see a large stone arch on the wall just outside this Flagellation Church, marking this station and flogging occurrence again.

The Chapel of the Condemnation and Imposition of the Cross

The Chapel of the Condemnation and Imposition of the Cross is easily recognized by the five white domes on top. It was a Byzantine church which memorializes where Jesus was brought to the judgment seat by the high priest to Pontius Pilate and is part of the Antonia Fortress. The chapel was built from 1857 to 1868 by a Jewish convert with remains from a fifth-century church. It features lovely papier-mâché figures that illustrate some of the events that occurred along the Via Dolorosa. The Roman Catholic Church currently maintains this compound.

According to tradition, the Chapel of Condemnation is situated where Jesus was scourged and bound to the cross. It's paved with large grooved slabs of stone—the Lithostratos, which constitutes part of the yard where Jesus was on trial. Some people claim that the actual sacred stairs—Scala Sancta—which Jesus descended from the Praetorium after His trial were transferred to Rome during the fourth century AD. I climbed those stairs on my knees, saying prayers all the way up with other pilgrims. Put that amazing city of Rome on your travel list too!

Flogging and Scourging

The first thing the Romans did to a prisoner who was condemned to be crucified was scourge him. Not wanting to upset the many followers of Jesus, it has been said that Pilate might have hoped a little scourging would appease the angry crowd and they could call it a day. After all, Pilate stated earlier that he had not found any fault in Jesus and thought He was innocent of any real crimes, certainly not any that would merit crucifixion.

Outside on the street where you just came from are some darker stones formed in nine semi-circles. Some believe that is the exact spot where Jesus was flogged, and with the mockery of a thorny bush, He was crowned the King of the Jews.

So, what's the difference between flogging and scourging? Flogging generally refers to repeated whipping across the accused person's back with something called a cat o' nine tails, usually made out of leather, rope, hemp, or rawhide. The name comes from the scratches left on a person's back, the nine cords symbolizing the nine lives of a cat. Deuteronomy 25:3 explains that a criminal can receive no more than forty lashes. So that the Jews would not break this command by accidentally counting incorrectly, it was customary to use thirty-nine lashes, which is probably what Jesus received. Technically, it was the Romans who flogged Jesus, not the Jews, so we simply don't know for sure.

Scourging takes it to another vicious and deliberately cruel level. Scourging was a very popular form of punishment in Roman times. It involved a whip called a "flagrum" or a "flagellum," which had leather thongs embedded with pieces of metal, stone, or bone, designed to cause maximum damage and pain. All the sharp edges would tear the accused's flesh, exposing broken skin and ripped muscle tissue, resulting in blood loss, bruising, swelling, and even death sometimes.

Isaiah 53:5 tells us why Jesus had to be scourged: "But he was wounded for our transgressions, he was bruised for our iniquities: the chastisement of our peace was upon him; and with his stripes we are healed." This certainly refers to our physical and spiritual healing.

First Peter 2:24–25 adds more clarity to the spiritual nature of Jesus's suffering: "Who his own self bares our sins in his own body on the tree, that we, being dead to sins, should live unto righteousness: by whose stripes ye were healed." Through His scourging, Jesus demonstrated His willingness to suffer both spiritually and physically for us. In a very real way, the Savior defeated both physical and spiritual death on the cross.

The stripes on matzah, the unleavened bread eaten during Passover, are traditionally understood by Christians to symbolize the scourging of Jesus Christ. Isaiah 53:5 prophesies that the Messiah would be "wounded for our transgressions" and "by His stripes we are healed" The baking process of matzah intentionally creates stripes and piercings on the bread, mirroring the physical afflictions Jesus endured.

Have you ever noticed that modern-day Matza bread has stripes on it? The ancient Israelites ate Matzah because they left in a hurry to escape captivity as slaves in Egypt, so they didn't have time to allow their bread to rise. Instead, they quickly made their dough and cooked it on a grate over the hot coals, which is what formed the stripes on the large crackers sold in stores today. To them, Matzah is a symbol of freedom.

In John 6:35, we are told that Jesus is "the bread of life." Could it be that Heavenly Father was trying to prepare the Jews to recognize their Messiah by the stripes He would receive as the Bread of Life? God gave them clues many times, yet many of them never recognized the messianic symbols.

When I was in Israel, I met a man who shared a touching story about this concept. While attending a Latter-day Saint sacrament meeting, he saw one of the priests preparing the sacrament drop a piece of bread on the ground. The priest tore the bread and put it in the tray with a shrug, not realizing anyone was watching. The man was shocked and decided he wouldn't partake of the sacrament that day. Then, he realized that he had previously learned how Christ's body was truly bruised and broken and yet He still gave it for us, willingly. So, he did take the sacrament bread that day (from the exact tray with the "tainted" bread) with deeper appreciation for the Savior.

When we partake of the bread and the water each week during sacrament meeting, we are reminded that Jesus gave everything for us, including His body and blood, to redeem us from physical and spiritual death. The priests preparing the trays on the wooden table at the front of the chapel should remind us of Jesus on the wooden cross. The white cloth that is placed over the trays of bread and water should vividly remind us how Christ's broken body was wrapped in linen and placed in the tomb. We should practically jump for joy in our pews to remember that because of those events, we have been redeemed!

The Cross

Many Christian tour groups can be seen walking through the Via Dolorosa today, taking turns carrying a large wooden cross. While the crosses are designed to not be too heavy, it's often difficult for the carriers to navigate the crowded, narrow streets of Old Jerusalem. Whenever I walk along especially narrow roads or stairs in Jerusalem, I think of 2 Nephi 9:41, which says, "Behold, the way for man is narrow, but it lieth in a straight course before him, and the keeper of the gate is the Holy One of Israel."

In artwork, we often see images of the cross Jesus bore with various letters like INRI. Eastern Orthodox religions display it with the Greek letters INBI. The initials INRI are in Latin, which translates in English to "Jesus the Nazarene, King of the Jews" (John 19:19). The Romans intended this to be a mocking title. Little did they know how true the statement was!

A whole cross would have weighed over three hundred pounds, but the crossbeam would have probably weighed less, about one hundred pounds. The horizontal beam was called the "patibulum," while the vertical beam was called the "stipes." The stipes most likely would have already been fixed in place at the execution site on Golgotha. The purpose of making Jesus carry part of the crucifixion cross through the city was purely for ridicule and additional suffering.

It is likely that the beam Jesus carried to Golgotha would have been made from a local tree like olive or pine, typical construction materials in that region at the time. In the Garden of Gethsemane, there are trees 926 years old. It would have been fitting and even poetically symbolic if Jesus's cross had come from that olive grove. We don't know the length of the cross, but it would have had to be tall enough to elevate Jesus's body for public display to humiliate Him.

While the Romans intended the cross to be used as torture and final judgment over Jesus, it has now become a worldwide symbol for Christians as a loving reminder that Jesus was the true victor that day, conquering death and sin.

Surprisingly, there are quite a few different crosses that are common in the Christian world.

Over the years, many of my friends have asked why members of The Church of Jesus Christ of Latter-day Saints don't wear decorative crosses on necklaces or T-shirts. Elder Jeffrey Holland once shared a great way to answer that question. He emphasized that "The Church of Jesus Christ of Latter-day Saints considers the atoning sacrifice of Jesus Christ to be the central fact, the crucial foundation, the chief

doctrine, and the ultimate expression of divine love in God's grand plan for the salvation of His children."[13] This goes with Joseph Smith's teaching that "all things which pertain to our religion are only appendages to the Atonement of Jesus Christ."[14]

More recently, President Gordon B. Hinckley stated, "I do not wish to give offense to any of my Christian brethren who use the cross on the steeples of their cathedrals and at the altars of their chapels, but for us, the cross is the symbol of the dying Christ, while our message is the declaration of the living Christ."[15]

Some people believe that the Atonement of Jesus Christ was designed to help us repent from big sins, but we need the Atonement daily, even for seemingly small mistakes. We also need it because Christ also suffered for all of our emotional pain and understands us perfectly. It wasn't until I was a young mother that I finally appreciated the part of the Atonement that applied directly to me. I had just lost a baby and my heart was broken.

Both my spirit and body grieved for the loss of my little one. I could hardly function and spent weeks in a dark depression. One afternoon, while I was listening to a church talk to try to calm my tormented soul, I felt the Savior's loving arms embrace me. I didn't feel His actual arms, but I *knew* He was right there next to me. I felt an overwhelming sense of love and peace. I knew that everything would be all right and that the Savior knew me, loved me, and was sad with me. The cleansing tears began to flow down my cheeks. It changed everything for me.

I suddenly remembered that part of the Atonement included the pains of the world that Jesus experienced in the Garden of Gethsemane, which were so great that He bled from every pore. He suffered for all our sins, but He also felt the weight of our troubles and sorrow from mortality—even those not connected with sin. He understood fully what it feels like to be mortal. I realized that Jesus *knew* exactly how I was feeling because He had felt it already before me. His Atonement washes over sins *and* the tears of mortal living. For the first time, the Atonement became very real to me.

Nephi refers to the Savior as "my Jesus" (2 Nephi 33:6). I learned that He is also *my* Jesus. His atoning sacrifice really was for *me*. I knew He could heal my heart and make my burden light. He was the only one who could do it.

After this experience, I had greater empathy and understanding for others who had lost their babies. I loved the children I did have even more. I wanted to be better. My trial seemed to shorten the distance between me and my Heavenly Father. I became instantly focused on what truly mattered in life. Would I wish that pain on anyone? Absolutely not, but I recognize the importance of the trial in teaching me some important lessons in life. Whatever your cross is in life (there will be many!), bear it well. Learn from it. Be thankful for the opportunity to learn and grow.

The Church of the Sisters of Notre Dame De Sion

Near the Ecce Homo arch that marks the second station is a special site that is not technically considered a station on the Via Dolorosa but offers a unique experience and adds insight to station 2. The entrance is near the corner of Via Dolorosa Street and a narrow alley called Adabat el-Rahbat, also called The Nuns' Ascent.

Don't miss this part of your Via Dolorosa experience. Many tourists wander right past it. For a few shekels, a guide will take you on a tour of the underground streets and reservoir called the Strouthion Pool, constructed by the Hasmoneans in the second century. It was even mentioned by the famous Jewish historian Flavius Josephus in his account of the siege of Jerusalem in *The Jewish War* (V, 457).

A canal used to provide water to the Temple Mount cisterns, but part of that waterway was destroyed when Herod built a moat around the Antonia Fortress. A water reservoir (the Strouthion Pool) was dug into the moat and later vaulted over. You can see those ruins and the water far below the street level today.

This area has been historically called Gabbatha, which means "elevated place" or "pavement." Many believe this provides sufficient evidence that this area is the correct location of Pontius Pilate's judgment of Jesus because John 19:13 mentions both Gabbatha and Pavement. Those first-century stones under the ground are pretty convincing, although many archeologists still disagree and believe Gabbatha might have been closer to Herod's Palace, which also served as a Roman administrative center at the time. That's how it is in Jerusalem: religious tradition vs. debated archeology.

Many traditions connect Gabbatha to the Lithostratos, the large stone pavement at station 2. The large flagstones include carvings that appear to be Roman game boards, possibly used by soldiers for entertainment. All four Gospel writers mentioned that the Roman soldiers played games during Jesus's crucifixion. Matthew 27:35 and Mark 15:24 specifically mention that the soldiers cast lots (similar to throwing dice) for Jesus's clothing, fulfilling the prophecy in Psalm 22:18. King David must have seen the Savior's crucifixion in vision when he wrote that.

A tour guide of the chapel will show you an area with stones they believe to be from Jesus's time, suggesting the Savior might have walked on those very stones. Our tour guide allowed us to take our shoes off and actually walk on the stones. Some people even write notes to the Savior and place them between the stones. It's a sobering experience. It's a fascinating tour and definitely worth your time.

If no tour guide from the chapel is available, you can read the many placards that explain what you see there. Plus, there is a restroom! (WC stands for "water closet," which is the British name for restroom.)

The pamphlet visitors are given when entering this site states that the nuns here have a special "charism," which means a special spiritual gift or grace given by the Holy Spirit to benefit the world. Their stated charism is to "give witness in the church and in the world to God's love for the Jewish people." Catholics believe charisms can include teaching, healing, leadership, prophecy, service, mercy, or even administration. You and I know them as gifts of the Spirit, as mentioned in 1 Corinthians 12:4–11 and Romans 12:6–8. We are encouraged to develop and even ask for gifts of the Spirit (1 Corinthians 12:31; 14:1). Which ones are you actively seeking and developing?

The Prison

While it isn't officially a part of station 2, I don't want you to miss the prison located next to the Ecce Homo Arch just past station 2 on the same street you're standing on. You will see a stone sign at the entrance that says, "Greek Orthodox Patriarchate of Jerusalem, Prison of Christ." The word "patriarchate" refers to the ecclesiastical office and jurisdiction of a patriarch.

The Greek Orthodox religion believes stations 1 and 2 are the true locations of the trial at the Praetorium spoken of in the Bible. Of course, this prison is yet one more site in Jerusalem that many scholars and archeologists disagree about. The Greek Orthodox church claims that Jesus stayed there as a prisoner, awaiting His trial. At the prison you can see the cave He was placed in and the holes where His legs were placed and chained on a bench. Ironically, Jesus did break the chains of spiritual and physical death. It's heartbreaking to imagine the Savior of the World being treated like such a criminal.

Walking down the stairs into the dungeon is a unique experience and one you should definitely do if you have the time. It doesn't take very long. Ephesians 4:9 says that Christ descended into the lower parts of the earth, and this dark cave of a prison absolutely feels like that scripture was fulfilled here. In Greek Orthodox tradition, this site marks the beginning of the Via Dolorosa.

Continuing on the Via Dolorosa Route

To continue to the next station on the Via Dolorosa, walk down the long street you've been on and then turn left on El Wad (Hagai) Road, a wider street also filled with markets and crowds. Be sure to look down at the corner because you will see large stones that have been dated to the Roman period from the first or second century. Because it's a corner of a busy intersection, you will often see modern-day soldiers with rifles literally standing on Roman pavement to guard the way.

Related Scriptures

Matthew 16:24

- The invitation is for anyone who is willing to humble himself and lovingly bear the cross of Jesus. Will you be His disciple?

John 19:4–5

- Pilate, having found no fault in Jesus, presents Him to the crowd after His scourging.
- Adorned with a crown of thorns and a purple robe, Pilate declares, "Behold, the man!"

Matthew 27:31–32

- After Jesus is mocked and beaten by the Roman soldiers, He is led away to be crucified.
- Simon of Cyrene is compelled to carry the cross for Jesus.

Mark 15:20–21

- Jesus is led out to be crucified after being mocked and beaten.
- Simon of Cyrene is forced to carry the cross for Him.

Luke 23:26

- As Jesus is led away, Simon of Cyrene is seized and made to carry the cross behind Jesus.
- This passage emphasizes Simon's role and Jesus's suffering.

John 19:1, 16–17

- Jesus carries His own cross to the place called Golgotha (Calvary), where He is crucified.
- Unlike the Synoptic Gospels, John focuses on Jesus initially carrying the cross Himself.

Isaiah 53:4–7:
While not explicitly mentioning the cross, this passage prophetically describes the suffering servant bearing the burdens of others.

Hebrews 12:2:

- Refers to Jesus enduring the cross, despising its shame, and focusing on the joy set before Him.

Deuteronomy 25:3

- The Jewish law of lashing is explained. In 2 Corinthians 11:24, we learn that Paul was lashed this way on five separate occasions.

Bring This Station to Life

Outside this compound on a wall on the street, a sign reads: "Matthew 16:24 states, 'Then said Jesus unto His disciples, If any man will come after me, let him deny himself, and take up his cross, and follow me.'" The invitation is for anyone who is willing to humble himself and lovingly bear the cross of Jesus. Will you be His disciple?

What a great thought for pilgrims to contemplate at the beginning of the Via Dolorosa journey. You're reading this book, so that makes *you* a pilgrim too. (You get all the perks without the foot blisters from all that walking!) As was the Roman custom, Jesus was forced to carry His own cross that He would be crucified on. For Him, it was a physical and a spiritual challenge.

When He asks us to take up our own cross, He's asking us to follow Him no matter what our challenges are, whether they be physical or spiritual. Make a list of all the challenges you have in your life right now. Is there anything about your challenges that would cause you to deny the Christ? If so, what could you do to stay true and follow Him?

If you're doing this exercise with a loved one, compare notes and determine how you might help each another in your trials. Jesus's friends and family walked the Via Dolorosa with Him. You can do the same for the people in your life who are struggling.

Suggested Hymns to Sing as a Family

187: God Loved Us, So He Sent His Son
188: Thy Will, O Lord, Be Done

CHAPTER 5

STATION 3
Jesus's First Fall

You will see the third station not far on your left. Next to it is the fourth station. Look for the small church entrance with an archway. This station's entrance features a touching bas-relief of Christ falling due to the weight of the cross. This intersection used to be dangerous, so you will most likely see military soldiers with machine guns standing around, something most of us are not used to seeing on our local streets.

The station marker explains that Jesus needed help carrying the cross, so it's assumed He had fallen. Did Jesus fall? When you walk on this Via Dolorosa pathway filled with uneven stones, you know it's entirely plausible and probable. I have tripped on those stones myself.

Jesus had been scourged and beaten, and He was trying to carry a heavy beam that would go on the cross once He reached Calvary. His head was bleeding from the crown of thorns crushed onto it, and He was tired, hungry, and thirsty. I can absolutely believe that He stumbled and fell. But where exactly did He fall? The scriptures don't tell us, but it is mostly through Catholic traditions that the three stations identifying a fall have been added to the Via Dolorosa route.

Also written on an archway over the marker are the words "Armenian Catholic Patriarchte." TE is the ninth letter of the Hebrew alphabet and is pronounced "tet" (rhymes with "mate"). The letter *tet* is Hebrew for "Christians." In Latin, it means "you."

You'll sometimes see an inscription with the letter TS, which is the eighteenth letter of the Hebrew alphabet has a "ts" sound (as in "nuts"). The letter was originally represented by a pictograph of a prostrate man.

On the entrance door, you will also see the Greek letters A and O (it looks like a horseshoe), which mean Alpha and Omega (the beginning and end). Alpha is the first letter of the Greek alphabet, and Omega is the last letter of the Greek alphabet. Alpha denotes that God is the first of all things (Revelation 22:13). He should also be the first, most important thing in our life.

The small chapel at station 3 was built during the fifteenth century and is currently maintained by the Armenian Catholic Church. You can go inside and see a large sculpture of Jesus struggling to carry the cross as He fell. There is an Armenian Quarter in Old Jerusalem, although this church is not in it. You are still in the Muslim Quarter. In 1947–48, just after World War II, this church was renovated with the financial assistance of the Polish army. Underground, you can access a cave that includes remains of a former Turkish bath.

The rocks on the pavement are said to have been where Jesus fell because they're from the Second Temple period.

We have all probably read and studied the life of Jesus many times and are familiar with the pains and sorrows He had to endure, yet we think, somehow, we can escape challenges in our own life. Elder Jeffrey R. Holland shared wise insights in a talk called "Waiting on the

Lord" in the October 2020 general conference: "One's life cannot be both faith-filled and stress-free. It simply will not work to glide naively through life, saying as we sip another glass of lemonade, 'Lord, give me all thy choicest virtues, but be certain not to give me grief, nor sorrow, nor pain, nor opposition. Please do not let anyone dislike me or betray me and, above all, do not ever let me feel forsaken by Thee or those I love. In fact, Lord, be careful to keep me from all the experiences that made Thee divine. And then, when the rough sledding by everyone else is over, please let me come and dwell with Thee, where I can boast about how similar our strengths and our characters are as I float along on my cloud of comfortable Christianity.'"

Christianity is comforting, but it is often not comfortable. President Russell M. Nelson said, "As part of the divine plan, we are tested to see whether we master weakness or let weakness master us."[16]

Related Scriptures

The Bible does not explicitly mention that Jesus fell while carrying the cross. However, the tradition of Jesus falling during the journey to Golgotha comes from Christian tradition, particularly through the Stations of the Cross, a devotional practice that commemorates Jesus's Passion and death. The falls are depicted in the third, seventh, and ninth stations, but these are not directly described in the Gospel accounts.

Scriptural Context

The Gospels describe Jesus carrying the cross and Simon of Cyrene being compelled to help, which may imply that Jesus struggled under the weight. We'll talk about Simon of Cyrene at another station that has been created in his honor.

Matthew 27:31–32

- Simon of Cyrene is forced to carry the cross, possibly indicating Jesus was unable to carry it further.

Mark 15:20–21

- Simon of Cyrene is compelled to carry the cross after Jesus is led out.

Luke 23:26

- Simon of Cyrene carries the cross behind Jesus, which could suggest Jesus needed assistance due to physical weakness.

John 19:17

- Jesus begins by carrying His own cross, but the other Gospels suggest Simon later takes over.

Non-Scriptural Traditions

The concept of Jesus falling during the Way of the Cross has been deeply ingrained in Christian piety and art. It reflects His humanity and the immense suffering He endured, even if it is not explicitly stated in the Bible.

Bring This Station to Life

A beautiful song called "Via Dolorosa" was written by Billy Sprague and Niles, published in 1983 by Capitol CMG. Sandi Patty made it popular when she sang it in English and Spanish. In an interview, she stated, "I think the challenge for a songwriter is always to find a new way to say the same story. When 'Via Dolorosa' came along my path, I was just blown away because it did just that. It told the story but in a new and fresh and incredibly artistic way."[17] Nowadays, you can easily find dozens of choirs and individuals singing it on YouTube. Watch some of them with your family.

Suggested Hymn to Sing as a Family

183: In Remembrance of Thy Suffering

CHAPTER 6

STATION 4
Jesus Meets His Mother

Station 4 is marked by the Armenian Catholic Church of Our Lady of the Spasm. I know the name sounds weird translated into English, but it refers to the emotional state of grief and sorrow on Mary's face when she saw her son carrying the heavy cross along the path while onlookers jeered and spat at Him (John 19:25–27). The original church on this site was built in the fifth century during the Byzantine period. You can still see a mosaic floor from that period down in the crypt. A newer church was built on the site in 1881.

There is a sweet sculpture below the arch outside the church that shows Jesus holding the cross, while His mother leans in to

provide comforting words and love. It was carved by the Polish artist Zieliensky. Inside the church is a large sculpture that illustrates the same love between the virgin mother and her divine son. A sign on the wall meant for tourists says, "Holy place. Please keep silence." A lovely mosaic on the floor dated from the fifth century depicts a pair of black sandals in its center. That exact location is believed by some Christians to be where Mary stood while watching her son.

Medieval pilgrims mentioned a church along the Via Dolorosa they called the Church of Our Lady of the Fainting that seems to be this same church. Around the inside walls of the church are paintings that illustrate each of the fourteen stations.

The New Testament tells us Mary was present at the crucifixion, so it's assumed she walked the path with her son on His final journey to fulfill His earthly mission. Many religions around the world are dedicated to Mary. Many worshippers pray to her to solicit her son's mercy. When I served my mission in Spain, I talked with many women who explained that they felt more comfortable praying to Mary because she was an approachable woman and mother like they were. Catholics pray to Mary while doing the rosary but do not worship her as God. Instead, they say the Hail Mary prayer and praise God for the wonderful things He has done in and through one of His creatures, and ask for her intercession on their behalf.

Like Mary, I am a mother. I have four sons and would do anything in my power to help them. Any mother would. The pure love of a mother is powerful and the closest thing to Christlike love on this earth. I can't even imagine how much Mary's heart was breaking as she witnessed her cherished son straining to carry the cross while dripping blood on every stone along the Via Dolorosa.

I can, however, imagine that she was remembering the baby she held to her breast, the young child who ran through the meadows near their house with joy, the teenager who taught her about her Father in Heaven, and the pride she must have felt as He began His glorious mission of healing and helping others. From her first encounter at the Annunciation, when she was told she had been chosen to be the mother of the Savior of the world, she knew where this painful path would lead. Luke 2:34–35 puts it well: "This child is destined for the falling and the rising of many in Israel. . . . And a sword will pierce your own soul too." Indeed.

Do you remember the part in the Book of Mormon that talks about the valiant stripling warriors and how they praised their mothers for having such strong faith? They attributed their success in battle to the teachings of their mothers. What a wonderful tribute. I love that the Via Dolorosa likewise honors a courageous woman who God described as "highly favored" (Luke 1:28).

When Mary was visited by the angel Gabriel, she was given information about her divine son, Jesus (Luke 1:26–56). The Annunciation marked the moment when God's plan to redeem humanity through Jesus began to unfold. From that moment, Mary knew her son had an important work to do. She had been taught about God her entire life and had personally experienced that God could send a messenger to convey His will for her. When Gabriel appeared to her, she apparently wasn't surprised. The scriptures don't say that she was frightened or shocked at the possibility.

Mary had great faith in God. She never doubted He was real. She never doubted His promises spoken by ancient prophets. During my mission, I learned how to connect people's faith in God and prophets to the Book of Mormon. Some of us missionaries would go to the parks in the early evenings when Spaniards love to take strolls with their families. We would set up tall sandwich boards with pictures of the plan of happiness and the restoration of the gospel on them. We called them *pancartas,* which translates as "banner" or "sign" used at public events.

My job was to wander through the park to strike up a conversation with passersby with the goal of inviting them back to the pancartas to learn more. I thought it was really fun to try to catch the attention of people as they walked by. Once I found interested people, I would walk them over to the pancartas and let the other missionaries continue the discussion. Then, I would run off and find some more people who might be interested in learning more.

One approach I often used to start a conversation with people was to ask them to answer five simple questions. People were intrigued by the specific number, so they would stop to chat. These are the five questions I would use.

1. Do you believe in God?
2. Do you believe He spoke anciently with prophets?
3. Do you believe God changes or is He always the same?
4. If you believe in God and that He spoke with prophets before and that He never changes, then is it possible that He could speak to prophets today?
5. If there were one of God's prophets on the earth today, would you want to know it and hear what he has to say?

It was fascinating to see the light bulb turn on in people's heads when they followed that logical sequence and honestly reflected on their answers. What are your answers?

The prophet Mormon tells us that God is "unchangeable from all eternity to all eternity" (Moroni 8:18). President Thomas S. Monson stated, "In this world where nearly everything seems to be changing, His constancy is something on which we can rely, an anchor to which we can hold fast and be safe, lest we be swept away into unchartered waters" ("Stand in Holy Places, October 2011 General Conference).

It takes practice to hear and recognize the voice of the Lord in our lives. The more we pray, the more we will hear Him. The more we live the principles we know to be true, the clearer His voice will be in our lives.

Sister Bonnie L. Oscarson, former Young Women General President, gave a great talk in the 2013 October 2013 general conference. She taught, "True conversion is more than merely having a knowledge of gospel principles and implies even more than just having a testimony of those principles. It is possible to have a testimony of the gospel without living it. Being truly converted means we are acting upon what we believe and allowing it to create "a mighty change in us, or in our hearts."

In the booklet *True to the Faith,* we learn that "conversion is a process, not an event. You become converted as a result of righteous efforts to follow the Savior." It takes time, effort, and work. The Lord invites us, "Draw near unto me and I will draw near unto you; seek me diligently and ye shall find me" (D&C 88:63). As we do so, we will feel His Spirit more abundantly in our lives. In today's crazy world, we need to hear God's will for us, whether those words come to us in prayer, through an angelic messenger, or a prophet.

Each day, we can be a little bit like Mary by showing our faith in a God who still speaks to us in prayer and through our living prophets.

Continuing on the Via Dolorosa Route

To continue the Via Dolorosa, keep walking down the same street you're already on. On your right, you will see the fifth station.

Related Scriptures

While there are no direct mentions of Mary witnessing Jesus carry the cross, she is present at the crucifixion, as noted in the following passages:

John 19:25–27

- "Near the cross of Jesus stood His mother, His mother's sister, Mary the wife of Clopas, and Mary Magdalene. When Jesus saw His mother there, and the disciple whom He loved standing nearby, He said to her, 'Woman, here is your son,' and to the disciple, 'Here is your mother.' From that time on, this disciple took her into his home."
- This shows Mary at the foot of the cross, witnessing her son's suffering and death.

Scriptural Mentions of Jesus's Journey to Golgotha

Luke 23:27–28

- This passage highlights women mourning for Jesus on His way to the cross, but Mary is not specifically mentioned.

Bring This Station to Life

Write a letter to your mother. Call her! Now would also be a good time to visit any widows in your ward or neighborhood.

Mothers hold a unique and irreplaceable role in our lives, shaping who we are with their love, sacrifices, and unwavering support. They are our first teachers, nurturing us with wisdom and instilling values that guide us through life. A mother's pure love is profound and unconditional, serving as a source of strength and comfort during our toughest times. Her sacrifices often go unnoticed, but they are the bedrock upon which families are built, offering patience, resilience, and an open heart that anchors us when the world feels uncertain.

As the poet Rudyard Kipling once said, "God could not be everywhere, and therefore he made mothers."[18] To celebrate mothers is to celebrate life itself.

Suggested Hymns to Sing as a Family

196: Jesus, Once of Humble Birth
Mary's Lullaby (*Children's Songbook,* 44).

CHAPTER 7

STATION 5
Simon of Cyrene Helps Jesus Carry the Cross

Station 5 is located in the Chapel of Simon of Cyrene on the corner of two narrow streets. It's marked with the Jerusalem cross as a bas relief on both sides of the door's entrance. The Jerusalem cross is unique to the Old City. It was designed by the Franciscan order and depicts a large cross with four smaller crosses in each corner at the top. It includes the intertwined arms of Jesus and St. Francis of Assisi at the bottom of the cross. You will see it everywhere in Jerusalem, often with just the crosses and no arms.

Two current theories attempt to explain the symbolism of the Jerusalem Cross. One proposes that the large cross represents Jesus Christ and the four smaller crosses represent the Gospel writers: Matthew, Mark, Luke, and John. The other theory suggests that the large cross represents Jesus's pierced heart, while the four smaller crosses represent Jesus's wounds on his hand and feet.

The events of this station are mentioned in Matthew 27:32, Luke 23:26, and Mark 15:21. The Roman soldiers recruited Simon of Cyrene (modern-day Libya) to help Jesus carry the cross. He was a passerby who was returning from the field with his children. The Latin inscription that is carved above the entrance to this station includes Simon's name and says "Cross Bearer."

To the right of the door, there is an indentation in the wall that is said to have been created in the stone when Jesus put His left hand there and rested against the wall for a moment. People visiting the spot often put their own hand over the stone to feel closer to Jesus. We can always feel closer to the Savior when we use our hands for good. Our goal should be to live in such a way that the Savior's image will be imprinted on us.

Christian tradition says that Jesus leaned against the stone wall when He saw the incline of the street to Golgotha. When we see difficult challenges coming our way, we can lean on the Savior. Don't you just love all this symbolism carved into the physical elements of the Via Dolorosa? Elder Ulisses Soares of the Quorum of the Twelve Apostles stated, "Symbolism, once understood, will give greater impact to that which we already know to be true, and it will make clear a greater unity among teaching and events found in Old Testament, the New Testament, and latter-day revelation."[19]

You can take a peek inside a small area that houses a sculpture representing this event. The small chapel was established by the Franciscans in 1229 and was their first site in Jerusalem.

Before this station was established to commemorate the aid Simon the Cyrene gave to Jesus, a fourteenth century tradition mentioned two other houses on this same corner. One of the houses belonged to the rich man mentioned in Luke 16:14–31, who refused to help the beggar, Lazarus. Another house on the corner was said to belong to Simon the Pharisee, where a sinful woman anointed the feet of Jesus, as mentioned in Luke 7:36–50. Today, those houses don't exist and there are no markers anywhere to identify them, but it's fun to imagine how things might have looked in Jesus's time.

I love that this station helps us focus on service to others. Focusing on others steadily bathes us with inspiration, motivation, and perspective. Whenever we are experiencing trials or feeling distanced from Heavenly Father, one of the best things we can do to get our perspective back is to serve. Happiness lies within us as we reach out to others. Happiness is not what you *get* but what you *give*.

When I was a young student at Brigham Young University, I volunteered as the student director at a night school for handicapped adults. Some of the people I taught were physically handicapped, but most of them were mentally handicapped and had severe learning disabilities. They lived in group homes where they had help with their everyday tasks, and they were attending night school to learn skills that would allow them to get a simple job in the community. I volunteered there twice a week and loved it. It was fun to teach the students, and I felt like I was doing something truly meaningful to help other people. After my second year of volunteering there, I often found myself frustrated because the students didn't seem to progress. I was a busy college student with my own challenges and worried that the time I spent would be better spent studying for my exams. I always felt great after serving at the school and knew it was good for me, but I wondered if I was making any real difference there. Even worse, I was in charge of all the other BYU student volunteers and worried that I might be wasting their time as well.

One Saturday morning, my parents came to town and took me out to breakfast. That was a real treat, and I was thrilled to spend a little bit of time with them. While we were eating, I noticed one of "my" mentally handicapped students sitting alone at a nearby table. I walked over and gave him a big hug. I asked him what he was doing there, and he informed me that it was his birthday. I was sad to see him sitting all by himself on such a special occasion, but he explained that he wanted to see if he could go to a restaurant by himself, order, and be like a "normal" person. He said that he had been inspired by our night classes together and he was challenging himself to become better.

I was so touched. I felt so much love for him, as well as for my Heavenly Father, who allowed me to serve such special people. My problems were never as large as I felt they were. I finally realized that we don't serve others to change the world but to change ourselves.

Simon of Cyrene's compelled act of carrying Jesus's cross exemplifies spontaneous service to others, highlighting how our unplanned assistance can often profoundly impact those in need. The scriptures tell us that Simon followed Jesus, offering another powerful example of what we need to do daily in our lives.

Continuing on the Via Dolorosa Route

To continue to the next station of the Via Dolorosa, turn to the right on El-Khanqa Street. You will immediately notice the steps on the path go up an incline toward Calvary. Be careful walking when there is dew or rain because the stone path gets slippery. The pavement you're now walking on is not from Roman times but is relatively new in modern-day times.

Related Scriptures

Matthew 27:32

- This passage highlights that Simon was compelled by the Roman soldiers to assist Jesus.

Mark 15:21

- Mark provides additional details about Simon, including the names of his sons, Alexander and Rufus, which suggests they were known to the early Christian community.

Luke 23:26

- Luke adds that Simon carried the cross "behind Jesus," emphasizing his role in following Jesus on the way to crucifixion.

Bring This Station to Life

Many opportunities to serve others are all around us. As a family, check out www.JustServe.org and find a simple project you could do in your community. If Jesus Christ were here today, that's what He would do!

Suggested Hymns to Sing as a Family

86: How Great Thou Art
223: Have I Done Any Good?

CHAPTER 8

STATION 6
Veronica Wipes the Face of Jesus

This station is marked by a brown wooden door and the same metal markers seen at other stations. You can also see Latin words carved into a column on the wall that detail what happened there. What makes the architecture visually outstanding is a series of flying buttresses above your head, across the station. Christian tradition from the fifteenth century states that a young woman named Veronica lived in that house and that Jesus cured her once before during His ministry. The story says that as Jesus walked the Via Dolorosa route, Veronica saw Him and rushed to wipe His bloody face with her veil. He was finally able to open His eyes better and was so grateful for the visual relief and act of mercy amidst so much brutality.

Later, when she looked at her cloth, she was able to see the image of Jesus's face imprinted on the fabric. This would be the first official Christian icon of Jesus Christ in history, *if* this story is true.

Folk etymology attributes the name Veronica to mean "true" or "truth" in Latin (vera) and "icon," which means "image" in Greek. Veronica means "true image" of Jesus. Others say her name is a symbol of her act of kindness.

Do Your Daily Acts Generate Images of Christ?

Veronica's cloth was on display in Constantinople (Istanbul) until the fifteenth century. When the Ottomans conquered Istanbul, the cloth disappeared. Catholics believe that the Veil of Veronica, also called Sudarium, is now kept by the Pope at the Vatican in Rome. Others believe that fragments of the cloth are being kept in various churches.

If people looked for fragments of Christ's image in you, would they be able to find evidence? Has His image been imprinted on you?

The 2004 movie *The Passion of the Christ,* directed by Mel Gibson, shows the tender moment between Veronica and Jesus, as well as Simon the Cyrene helping the Savior carry the cross to Calvary. The R-rated movie is incredibly brutal to watch because of its painfully realistic portrayal of what happened on the Via Dolorosa. Jesus absolutely needed their help. It's unbelievable that He even survived the barbaric scourging to get to the cross. In Roman times, some prisoners didn't last after that part of their merciless punishment.

One of the unique elements of the film is that the only languages spoken are Aramaic (Jesus and His disciples), Latin (the Romans), and Hebrew (the Jews) to add even more authenticity. The film is extremely well done with impressive details, but it's not for the faint of heart.

There is another legendary story that illustrates the importance of looking for the visage of the Savior in our daily lives. It's about the famous Italian painter Leonardo da Vinci. Some children were visiting the famous artist one day when one of them accidentally knocked over a stack of canvases. The master artist was upset because he had been working very quietly and sensitively. He instantly became angry, threw his brush on the floor, and hurled some harsh words at the frightened little boy, who ran crying from the studio. Leonardo was now alone again, and he began to continue his work. He was trying to paint the face of Jesus on the canvas that would become the famous work of art known as *The Last Supper,* but he couldn't do it. His creativity was gone.

Leonardo da Vinci put down his brush and went out into the streets and alleys until he found the little boy. He said, "I'm sorry, little one. I shouldn't have spoken so harshly. Forgive me, even as Christ forgives. I have done something worse than you. You only knocked over the canvases but I, in my anger, blocked the flow of God into my life. Will you come back with me?" He took the boy back into the studio with him. They smiled as the face of Jesus came quite naturally from the master's brush. That face has been an inspiration to millions ever since.

While we can't verify if the stories of Veronica or Leonardo da Vinci are true, they both teach us important lessons about looking to Christ every day.

Today, there is a small Greek chapel underground at the site of station 6 that marks the home of Veronica. It's called the Church of the Holy Face and Saint Veronica, and was built on the twelfth-century ruins by Greek Catholics in 1883.

Any time you have the opportunity to go underground in Jerusalem, take it because those layers get you closer to the original structures that existed during Jesus Christ's time. A placard in the chapel proudly states, "On January 4, 1964, His Holiness Pope Paul VI on pilgrimage to the Holy Land, prayed in this place where tradition commemorates the meeting of Veronica with Christ."

There is also a small workshop at the entrance of the church where nuns called the "Little Sisters of Jesus" create paintings of Jesus to sell them. What a sweet title to be given: a little sister of Jesus.

At this station, we learn that you don't have to wait for a formal assignment to do good. No one asked Veronica to provide comfort to the Savior. No one told her to be prepared with a cloth to wipe His face. She saw a need and took care of it.

I learned an important lesson about taking care of needs when I worked as an intern for a congressman in Washington, DC. I had great hopes of changing the world and thought of myself as the girl version from the inspirational movie *Mr. Smith Goes to Washington.* I really wanted to make a difference and prove that I was a deep thinking, valuable contributor to our country.

Each week a different person was chosen as intern of the week. I had no idea what that meant, but the title sounded very impressive. Then, the long-awaited day I arrived. I was told that I had been chosen as the intern of the week. I was thrilled, although I still didn't know what the honor meant. I learned the first part of my assignment was to arrive an hour early, open the office, prepare the congressman's office, go through the mail that had gathered overnight, and get the rest of the office ready for the day. I was so excited that I arrived two hours early. I just knew that this would be my week to shine. After I had finished the assigned tasks, I still had a half hour before anyone would arrive at the office.

I noticed the office bathroom and kitchenette were pretty dirty because no one in the office ever had time to clean, so I decided to straighten things up and do some extra cleaning. When the congressman arrived and saw what I had done, he was completely amazed and couldn't stop talking about it. You would have thought I had cured cancer or balanced the national budget by how much he praised me. All this time I had been trying to impress him with my clever mind and political acumen, only to finally catch his attention because I was willing to do some extra things like clean the toilet. Of course, I hadn't done it for the praise. What happened next amazed me.

Because of my willingness to do something no one else in the office would do, the congressman invited me to represent him at some incredible events during my time there. It was such an honor, and I was humbled that I had earned such trust. He was Jewish but knew about The Church of Jesus Christ of Latter-day Saints. When I asked him if he could speak to a group of BYU students, he left the floor during a live session in the House of Representatives to do so.

I learned a great lesson. You don't have to be told to do something in order to take action. Look for a need and meet it. It doesn't have to be your job or your calling. Be a Veronica. Let the Savior's image show in your countenance and behavior.

Continuing on the Via Dolorosa Route

Keep walking on this street. Look for the intersection of the Via Dolorosa with Khan es-Zeit (the Oil Market).

As you pass more shops along the street, you might notice that many of them sell jewelry that features the famous Eilat Stone, a blue-green gemstone also known as the King Solomon Stone. It is the national gemstone of Israel, named after the city of Eilat, where it was first discovered in the 1950s near the Red Sea. It has been associated with King Solomon's mines from biblical times, although those claims haven't been verified by historical evidence. It's absolutely gorgeous to look at, but it's also believed to have some metaphysical properties, including healing, balance, and tranquility. The claims have not been scientifically proven either but have definitely led to the stone's popularity and use with alternative therapies.

Related Scriptures

While there is no mention of the event with Veronica in the Bible, a similar story appears in the New Testament apocrypha about a post-Crucifixion "Holy Face" image attributed to the famous Shroud of Turin.

The history of the Shroud of Turin is fascinating. It's a cloth that bears the faint image of a man who appears to have been crucified. It measures about 14 feet by 3.5 feet and shows front and back images of a man with wounds consistent with crucifixion, including marks on the wrists, feet, and head (interpreted as from a crown of thorns).

Many Christians believe it is the burial shroud of Jesus Christ, making it one of the most studied and controversial religious relics in history. The Shroud of Turin continues to be a subject of extensive scientific investigation, with recent studies offering new insights and reigniting debates about its origin and authenticity. Recent testing in 2024 showed a bloodstain analysis that concluded the results were consistent with the torture and crucifixion as described in the Gospels. X-ray analysis in 2024 of the shroud's fibers showed evidence that the cloth could date back to the time of Jesus, debunking an old analysis that the shroud was from the Middle Ages. Another study in 2024 showed that an extremely bright light may have been the cause of the imprint.[20]

For believers, the shroud represents physical evidence of Jesus's death and resurrection. For skeptics, it's an artifact that might have been created as a devotional object or forgery. Currently, the Shroud of Turin is kept in the Cathedral of Saint John the Baptist in Turin, Italy. It is stored in a special climate-controlled case to prevent further deterioration. Public viewings are rare and draw large crowds when scheduled.

I don't know if the Savior's face really is on the Shroud of Turin, but I know that we can't put our faith in relics and religious objects. Our testimony must be firmly cemented in Jesus Christ.

An appropriate scripture for this station could be Numbers 6:24–26, which is often called the Priestly Blessing or Aaronic Blessing. It says:

> The Lord bless thee, and keep thee:
> The Lord make his face shine upon thee, and be gracious unto thee:
> The Lord lift up his countenance upon thee, and give thee peace.

Bring This Station to Life

A common practice among Latter-day Saint mission presidents is to challenge their missionaries to actively look for miracles each day. It's no surprise that thousands of missionaries are seeing miracles every day. We see what we look for. Is God walking with you, yet you don't even recognize His hand in your life?

Keep a "miracles" journal. Write down the everyday miracles in your life, large and small. When you're feeling as if the Lord has forgotten about you, read the entries in your journal to remind you how much He loves you.

Suggested Hymns to Sing as a Family

188: Thy Will, O Lord, Be Done
270: I'll Go Where You Want Me to Go

CHAPTER 9

STATION 7
Jesus's Second Fall

Look up to see the marker on the stone wall of the souq (market). This particular street is one of the busiest in the Old City, serving as an intersection of the Cardo Maximus and a transverse street of the Roman Aelia-Capitolina. Today, it's an intersection of the Via Dolorosa with Khan es-Zeit (the Oil Market), filled with shops and people. It is still a main artery of the city's bustling streets that runs from Damascus Gate to Zion Gate. In the Savior's day, the indictments of those condemned to death were published and hung on this site for the public to see.

This station marks the place where Jesus passed through the Gate of Judgment to the site of the crucifixion, which was outside of the city

walls at the time. The station marker is next to a Franciscan chapel built in 1875. Below the Franciscan chapel are some Roman remains dating back to the first and second century.

If the door by the station marker is open, you can step inside to see a column that is dated to the Roman period of the first or second century. There is also a small altar next to it, a Roman stone on the floor in front of it, and, often, someone who can answer questions for you.

It is said that Jesus tripped over the threshold, falling for the second time. Simon of Cyrene had been carrying the cross for Jesus (station 5), so who was actually holding the cross at this point? The scriptures don't tell us, nor does the Catholic tradition; however, we do know that Jesus had been brutally beaten all night long prior to being officially condemned (station 1) and must have been completely exhausted. By now, Simon might have been exhausted too. Perhaps they carried the cross together. Although we don't know, there are important lessons to be learned here.

I'm sure Jesus wanted to give up at this point, but He didn't. He knew His work wasn't finished yet, so He kept taking one step at a time, no matter how long it took. He showed us dedication to purpose and how to be persistent. There is no evidence that He complained and whined about the hard things He had to do. That was never His nature. Sometimes, we just have to go through challenging times; complaining doesn't help or change the circumstances. Elder Jeffrey Holland stated, "To be a follower of Jesus Christ, one must sometimes carry a burden and go where sacrifice is required and suffering is inevitable."[21]

Where Jesus is said to have tripped is where the city ended at that time. Jesus was leaving the busy city filled with many distractions. An interesting parallel is how some people can trip spiritually when they are wrapped up in worldly things. Today, that might refer to how much people focus on worldly trappings like cell phones, social media, acquiring money and material objects, mindless entertainment, or seeking the world's attention and fame.

This gate where Jesus fell the second time has been called many names throughout history. The Jews in Jerusalem often refer to it as the Gate of Jehoshaphat because it leads to Jehoshaphat Valley, where Rabbi Benjamin Tudela worshipped God in the twelfth century. After the Byzantine period, the gate was renamed Bab el-Ghor (the Jordan Valley gate), but people rarely use that name now.

It's also called the Lions' Gate because sculptures of four lions adorn the gate. Suleiman, one of the Muslim leaders who captured Jerusalem, had a dream that lions were attacking the city, so he built this gate for protection and added the images of the lions. Another tradition says that Suleiman dreamed he was going to be eaten by lions if he didn't build this part of the city. Ironically, Jesus, often called the Lion of Judah, claimed Jerusalem as His own and will return there.

The Sheep Gate

A gate is an entryway or exit, and was often called a threshold anciently. It sounds like Jesus literally tripped over the stones at the gate. In many religions, gates are considered to connect the living with the dead. Walking across the city's threshold, Jesus was literally leaving His mortal life and marching toward His imminent mortal death.

It is believed that Jesus walked through the Sheep Gate in Jerusalem like a lamb to the slaughter on His way to Golgotha. Back then, the gate led to the sheep market and was used for bringing sheep into the city for sacrifice in the Second Temple. Later, Sheep Gate was also called Stephen's Gate because it was through this gate that Stephen was martyred, according to Christian tradition (Acts 7:54–60).

There is so much rich symbolism at this one gate. We are like the sheep that must follow our shepherd, Jesus Christ. Sheep are known to be quite docile at the time of their slaughter, remaining quiet and submissive. Jesus never ranted or yelled or fought against His fate (Acts 8:32; Isaiah 53:7). He knew He was born for this role, and He willingly gave His life for each of us.

Jesus leads us to the temple where we sacrifice our broken heart and contrite spirit. The gate leads to the final cross; following the cross leads us to Jesus and eternal salvation. Jesus is the Lamb of God who takes away the sins of the world.

King David's life foreshadowed Jesus, the Good Shepherd (John 10:11, John 1:29). As a young boy, David was a shepherd to his family's flocks; as a man, he shepherded his nation as their king. David even wrote about Jesus's life as the Good Shepherd in Psalm 23:1, proclaiming "The Lord is my shepherd." Jesus knew that the Pascal lamb needed to be sacrificed at Passover, and He was the Lamb of God to be sacrificed. The prophecies would be fulfilled in Christ. He tried to remind the disciples to be good shepherds to His people who would feel like lost lambs after His death, saying, "Feed my sheep" (John 21:15–16).

Ancient tradition has identified King David's tomb at a specific site in Jerusalem. Because King David founded Jerusalem, Jews have flocked to where his tomb is currently located in the Old City to honor the greatest of their kings. Jesus probably visited there too! When the Jews were denied access to the Western Wall, they would go to the rooftop of the memorial for King David in order to see the Temple Mount.

King David's birth in Bethlehem is another link to Jesus that foreshadows His divine mission. And one of the sites that people claim is the Upper Room where Jesus held the Last Supper is above the site of King David's tomb. That symbolic location would have been perfect to hold such a significant event in Jesus's life. Christian tradition claims the Upper Room is at the Cenacle on Mount Zion, currently a popular site that pilgrims visit. The structure dates to the Crusader and later Ottoman periods, but it is believed to sit over or near the original location of the biblical event. Archaeological evidence suggests that the area had Jewish homes and was part of the upper-class quarter during Jesus's time, making it a plausible setting for the Last Supper.

Passover

Remember that the last hours of Jesus Christ's life occurred during the Passover (Pesach) season, which made Jerusalem extremely crowded and busy during the seven days of preparation and feasting. Passover is an annual holiday for Jews in the spring that commemorates the liberation of the Israelites from slavery when they were in Egypt. In the time of Jesus, the Jews were free yet still slaves to taxes and the strong arm of the Romans.

The name "Passover" refers to the tenth and final plague that God inflicted upon Egypt—killing the firstborn of every household—when God "passed over" the homes of the Israelites who had marked their doorposts with lamb's blood as instructed. Jesus was now very close to being that sacrificed lamb, shedding His blood to save us all. He has been called the "Firstborn" (Luke 2:7; Colossians 1:15–18; Romans 8:29; Hebrews 1:6) and the "Firstfruits" (1 Corinthians 15:20–23; Romans 8:23; James 1:18). Did the Jews see and understand that connection? Some did. Sadly, many did not.

Passover is not only a commemoration of freedom from physical slavery but also a reflection on personal and spiritual liberation. It encourages themes of gratitude, faith, and resilience for the Jews. While not a "High Holy Day," Passover is one of the three Pilgrimage Festivals (Shalosh Regalim), along with Shavuot (Festival of Weeks) and Sukkot (Festival of Booths). These festivals were historically times when Jews would travel to the temple in Jerusalem to offer sacrifices and celebrate communally. Passover begins on the fifteenth day of the Hebrew month of Nisan, typically falling in March or April on the Gregorian calendar.

The Jews revere Moses for saving their people. Moses is considered a type and a shadow of Christ in Christian theology because many aspects of his life, role, and mission prefigure and foreshadow the person and work of Jesus Christ. A "type" in biblical typology refers to a person, event, or institution in the Old Testament that serves as a prophetic symbol pointing to a greater fulfillment in the New Testament.

For example:

- Moses delivered the Israelites from physical slavery (Exodus 3:10). Jesus delivers mankind from spiritual slavery caused by sin (John 8:34–36; Romans 6:6).
- Moses served as a mediator of the old law and covenant between God and Israel by presenting the Ten Commandments given to Him on Mount Sinai (Exodus 19–24). Jesus mediated the new covenant by fulfilling the law and introducing the higher covenant through the gospel (Hebrews 8:6; Luke 22:20).
- Moses interceded for Israel when they sinned, asking God for mercy (Exodus 32:11–14). Jesus continually intercedes for us before God and will stand at the final judgment with us (Hebrews 7:25; Romans 8:34).
- Moses was considered a great prophet who spoke God's words

(Deuteronomy 18:15). Jesus *is* the Word and fulfilled the prophecy Moses foretold about Him (John 7:16; Acts 3:22–26).

- Moses performed miracles to demonstrate God's power (Exodus 14:21; Numbers 20:8). Jesus performed even greater miracles to demonstrate God's love (Mark 4:39; John 11:43).
- Moses was initially rejected by the Israelites, who questioned his leadership (Exodus 2:14; Numbers 14:4). Jesus was rejected by His people, even to death (John 1:11; Luke 23:18).
- Moses led the Israelites to the edge of the promised land (Deuteronomy 34:4–5). Jesus leads believers to the ultimate promised land—eternal life in the kingdom of heaven (John 14:2–6).

The highlight of Passover is the seder meal, held on the first (and often second) night of the holiday. During the seder, the Jews read the Haggadah, a special text that recounts the Exodus story when the Israelites were slaves in Egypt. The seder meal is highly symbolic and ritualistic. If you ever get an invitation to participate in a seder, do it! I have attended several and thoroughly enjoyed the experiences.

While the Jews focus on foods that cause them to remember the suffering of their people as slaves in Egypt and being saved by God through Moses, Christians can readily see how the symbols simultaneously represent Jesus Christ. For example, part of the meal includes eating matzah, as discussed in chapter 4. Jews eat matzah instead of leavened bread during Passover to remember that the Israelites had to leave Egypt so quickly that their bread did not have time to rise. Quickly cooking the bread crackers over a hot grill seared "stripes" on the top. Those stripes remind us of the Old Testament prophecy that through Jesus's stripes we are healed (Isaiah 53:5).

But there is even more to the matzah than that. A fun Jewish tradition at the seder is called the "afikoman," which is when a piece of matzah is broken, hidden inside a cloth, and then found later to eat at the end of the meal. Jesus's body was on the cross, then wrapped in a linen, and later appeared when He was resurrected. During the meal, Jewish families pass around the hidden piece of matzah under the table to each other. At the end of the meal, whoever has it in their hands has to do what everyone else at the table wants them to do. I happened to be the one with the matzah on my lap at the end of the first seder I went to, so I was a bit nervous to see what everyone was going to make me do. I was on a date with a man at the dinner, so everyone decided that I had to kiss him. We weren't a couple, so it was kind of awkward but all in good fun.

In some families, the leader of the seder meal, usually the father, hides the matzah somewhere in the room. Then the children have to hunt for it and receive a prize like candy or money. Christians know that we all have to find Jesus in our lives and that the true prize is eternal salvation.

Before Passover, Jewish households remove chametz (all leavened products) from their homes as a symbolic act of spiritual cleansing. They obey the letter of the law, as their Torah includes 613 commandments (Mitzvot) they strictly follow all year long. Jesus taught us to live the higher law by removing the world from our hearts.

The seder also includes eating bitter herbs called maror to remind the Jews of the bitterness of slavery that their ancestors endured in Egypt (Exodus 12:8). Today, Jews often eat horseradish, endive, parsley, or the stems of romaine lettuce, dipping the tips in vinegar to symbolize the tears of the Israelites. Christians interpret the symbolism of the bitter herbs as the bitterness of sin and the suffering Jesus endured for humanity on the cross, as well as in the Garden of Gethsemane.

On the seder plate is a lamb shank bone (zeroa) that symbolizes the Paschal lamb that was sacrificed and whose blood was placed on the doorposts during the Exodus. We know Jesus is the Lamb of God who sacrificed His life to pay for the sins of mankind (John 1:29).

Charoset is often everyone's favorite part of the seder meal because it is a sweet mixture of apples, nuts, and wine, symbolizing the mortar used by the Israelites in slavery when they had to build the Pharaoh's monuments and buildings. Jesus was building the kingdom of God during His mission, and the sweetness is seen as the hope and promise of salvation through His Atonement. He invites us to join His kingdom.

Four cups of wine (or grape juice for children) are served during the seder meal to remind Jews of the four promises of redemption spoken of in Exodus 6:6–7. Christians link this symbol to the wine at the Last

Supper when Jesus taught the disciples it represented His blood that would be shed for the new covenant (Luke 22:20).

A hard-boiled or roasted egg (beitzah) is also placed on the seder plate to symbolize how hard it has been to lose the temple in Jerusalem. It's a symbol of mourning, but in Christianity, it's a symbol of renewal and rebirth. Some say this Jewish tradition is what spawned the popularity of Easter eggs in modern Christianity.

God set all of these things in place in Old Testament times so that when Jesus appeared, the Jews would recognize Him. The symbolism is rich and delicious to our souls.

Continuing on the Via Dolorosa Route

If you are visiting Jerusalem in the fall and enter the Old City through the Lions' Gate, be sure to purchase some fresh almonds just outside the gate because that is the time of year when they are the freshest. You've probably never seen a fresh almond like this before. It's eaten in its soft skin and tastes like no almond you've never tasted before.

You are now slowly entering the Christian Quarter of the city; however, the streets still look quite Muslim with all of their shops. This area is called a "souk," which means bazaar or marketplace in Arabic. Look for the halva shop. Halva is a Middle Eastern confectionery that is made of sesame seed paste, sugar, spices, and nuts (in Arabic, "halva"

means "sweetness"). It's both crumbly and creamy at the same time, served as slices or squares from a decorative block loaf, and comes with a variety of other ingredients to choose from. It doesn't require refrigeration, which is why it's so popular all over the Middle East.

Next, turn left onto Beit-Habad Street, which is at the corner of station 7. Along the left side of the street is the German hospice of Saint John, decorated with the Maltese cross, the heraldic cross of the Order of St. John, also known as the Knights Hospitallers. The eight points of the cross represent the eight obligations of the order, which include loyalty, piety, honesty, courage, honor, faith, charity, and respect for the church. The Maltese cross is a symbol of the fire service today.

While not specifically mentioned in the Bible, the Maltese cross has come to symbolize the beatitudes in Jesus's Sermon on the Mount (Matthew 5:3–12), as well as the eight days from Christ's death to His appearance to His apostle "doubting" Thomas (John 20:26).

Keep walking down that street and look for marker 8 on the left wall.

Related Scriptures

The Via Dolorosa includes the tradition of Jesus falling three times during His walk to Golgotha. This idea isn't scriptural; however, it should give us hope and reassurance to know that we can fall spiritually many times, and the Savior will lift us up each time. He will never give up on us.

The third station commemorates the first fall, the seventh station commemorates the second fall, and the ninth station commemorates the third fall. These are not explicitly mentioned in the Gospels but have been adopted into Christian tradition to emphasize Jesus's suffering.

Related Scriptures

John 5:2

- John mentions the Sheep Gate.

Revelation 5:5–6

- The Lion of Judah is mentioned.

Bring This Station to Life

Jesus taught the Apostles that He would die and be resurrected after three days, but they didn't fully understand His message because no one had ever done that before. No one had ever seen it before.

To help you and your family better visualize some of the events that took place on the Via Dolorosa, consider watching a movie that illustrates the touching scenes. Of course, the ages of your family members will need to be considered because some of these films are quite graphic, showing torture, blood, and death. Here are some suggestions:

Children (animated and gentle)

- *Veggie Tales: An Easter Carol*
- *Come Follow Me*
- *The Lion of Judah*
- *The Easter Promise*
- *The Greatest Adventures of the Bible: The Easter Story*
- *The Witness*
- *The Easter Story Keepers*
- *The Animated Passion Trilogy (He is Risen, Worthy Is the Lamb, The Kingdom of Heaven)*
- *The Miracle Maker*
- *Heaven Is for Real*

Teenagers

- *The Gospel of John* (also marketed as *The Visual Bible: John*)
- *The Robe*
- *The Chosen* (season 6 shows the crucifixion)
- *The Young Messiah*
- *Ben-Hur*
- *Risen*
- *King of Kings*
- *The Greatest Story Ever Told*
- *Jesus of Nazareth* (TV series)
- *The Jesus Film*
- *Son of God*
- *The Life of Jesus*
- *Last Days in the Desert*
- *The Gospel of John*
- *The Gospel According to Saint Matthew*
- *Jesus* (You can see a free movie called *Jesus* that features the stations and Simon the Cyrene at http://jfp.org.watch. A docudrama on the life of Jesus Christ based on the Gospel of Luke, *Jesus* has been translated into more than one thousand languages since its 1979 release. It remains the most translated and viewed film in history. Since 1979, The Jesus Film Project has been known for its diverse library of gospel-centric media that brings people face to face with Jesus.)

Adults Only

- *The Passion of the Christ* (This is rated a hard R for its very realistic portrayal of how Jesus was flogged, beaten, and crucified. Mel Gibson just finished writing the sequel to this movie with his brother and will begin filming *The Passion of the Christ: Resurrection* in 2025.)

Suggested Hymns to Sing as a Family

108: The Lord Is My Shepherd
189: O Thou, Before the World Began

CHAPTER 10

STATION 8
Jesus Consoles the Crying Women

The site of the eighth station bears a sign on a stone wall on the left side of the street. Look closely or you'll miss it! Look for a similar round metal marker and sculpture that have identified the previous stations. Next to the marker is what looks like an old Roman column, sliced and placed on its side on the wall. The inscription on it says, "ICXC NIKA," which comes from Greek and means "Jesus Christ, the victor!" or "Jesus Christ conquers."

The Roman column at the site was reused when the Greek Orthodox church built a monastery there. That monastery wall blocks the path that would have directly led to Golgotha. Behind this wall is the Church of the Holy Sepulchre, which contains stations 10 through 14, but you can't get there that way anymore. (Don't worry! I'll take you there soon enough.) This is a perfect example of how the current Via Dolorosa route is probably not the exact way Jesus went to Calvary but is mostly based on Medieval traditions. Still, many of the locations are considered plausible and pretty close to the real locations.

Station 8 of the Via Dolorosa is the traditional site where Jesus addressed the daughters of Jerusalem when they were weeping about His fate in Luke 23:27–31. Jesus urged them to focus on the future and not just His present suffering. The women were tearful because they knew Jesus was going to be crucified. Jesus told them they should really be crying for their own fate and for that of their children because Jerusalem would be destroyed again (Luke 19:43–44). It's no surprise that it was destroyed by the Romans in AD 70, about forty years after Jesus was crucified.

In Bible numerology, the number forty signifies a trial that offers preparation and transformation for something better. For example, the rain fell for forty days and nights while Noah and his family were in the ark (Genesis 7:12). The Israelites wandered in the desert for forty years after leaving Egypt as slaves (Numbers 14:34). Moses fasted for forty days before receiving the Ten Commandments from God on Mount Sinai (Exodus 34:28). Jesus was tempted by Satan in the wilderness for forty days and nights before officially beginning His mission (Matthew 4; Luke 4; Mark 1). There were forty days between Jesus Christ's resurrection and ascension (Acts 1). I love how God embeds lessons and symbolic images inside the numbers He uses with events to help us better understand the nature and purpose of those events.

Jesus shifted the focus from His own suffering to the future tribulations that would come upon Jerusalem, a city that was near and dear to His heart. His words about the barren being blessed and people wishing for death (Luke 23:29–30) refer to the coming destruction of Jerusalem. In verse 31, Jesus mentions a green tree and a dry tree. The green tree symbolizes Jesus's innocence and the righteous suffering He is enduring. The dry tree symbolizes the judgment that will come upon those who reject Him. His words suggest that if people treat the innocent (Him) this way, how much worse will it be for those who are guilty?

Wars. Rumors of wars. Plagues. Pestilence. Famine. We live in the last days before Christ comes again. These are scary times but also exciting times. You are going to see some amazing things in your lifetime. You will see prophecies fulfilled. It's going to be epic. Wait, it already *is* epic!

I often wonder if our ancestors are looking down in awe and wishing they could have been born during this fascinating time in the world's history. Some of them are certainly jealous that we get cell phones *and* Snickers candy bars.

You have been selected to be here now. The Lord knows you and what you can do. He needs you to be one of the valiant ones He can count on.

Ezra Taft Benson said in 1987, "In all ages, prophets have looked down through the corridors of time to our day. Billions of the deceased and those yet to be born have their eyes on us. Make no mistake about it—you are a marked generation. There has never been more expected of the faithful in such a short period of time than there is of us. Never before on the face of this earth have the forces of evil and forces of good been as well organized. Now is the great day of the devil's power. But now is also the great day of the Lord's power, with the greatest number ever of priesthood holders on the earth. For nearly 6000 years, God has held you in reserve to make your appearance in the final days before the Second Coming of the Lord. Some individuals will fall away, but the kingdom of God will remain intact to welcome the return of its head—even Jesus Christ. While our generation will be comparable in wickedness to the days of Noah, when the Lord cleansed the earth by flood, there is a major difference this time. It is that God has saved for the final inning some of His strongest children, who will help bear off the kingdom triumphantly. That is where you come in, for you are the generation that must be prepared to meet your God."[22] That's such an incredibly powerful quote, promise, and challenge.

Neal A. Anderson reminded us in the April 2014 general conference that "the world will not glide calmly to the Second Coming." What does that mean? It's going to be a bumpy ride, and you get to be on it! When the winds howl around us, whether physical or spiritual, we need to stand firmly on the rock of our Redeemer.

As the prophet Elisha taught, unseen hosts watch over us. In 2 Kings 6, the nation of Israel was surrounded by enemies. One of the servants of the prophet Elisha was frightened and asked, "Alas, my master! How shall we do?" (That's kind of like saying, "EEK! What do we do now?" Elisha calmly declared, "Fear not: for they that be with us are more than they that be with them." The prophet then prayed that the Lord would open this young man's eyes, and when He did, the servant saw that the mountain near them was full of horses and chariots of fire to protect Israel. If you believe the scriptures, then you believe the Lord can protect you too.

Peace comes not from the absence of conflict in life but from the ability to deal with it. Sometimes the unexpected happens and ruins your plans. But sometimes life has pleasant surprises too.

You can't control the length of your life—
But you can control its width and depth
You can't control the contour of your face—
But you can control its expression
You can't control the weather—
But you can control the atmosphere of your mind
Why worry about the things you can't control
When you can keep yourself busy controlling the things that depend on you![23]

Leo Buscaglia, a popular writer in the 1980s, once said, "It's time to stop saying you're at the mercy of forces greater than you. . . . You are the greatest force upon yourself!"[24] The Lord will punish the wicked and test the valiant, so you're not getting out of trials either way.

"Every calamity that can come upon mortal beings will be suffered (allowed) to come upon the few, to prepare them to enjoy the presence of the Lord. If we obtain the glory that Abraham obtained, we must do so by the same means that he did. If we are ever prepared to enjoy the society of Enoch, Noah, Melchizedek, Abraham, Isaac, and Jacob, or of their faithful children, and of the faithful Prophets and Apostles, we must pass through the same experience, and gain the knowledge, intelligence, and endowments that will prepare us to enter into the celestial kingdom of our Father and God. Every trial and experience you have passed through is necessary for your salvation."[25]

Some people get scared or depressed when they think about all of the horrible things that are going to happen in the future. There once was a family who was pulling weeds in their backyard. Everyone was grumbling and complaining. Suddenly, they noticed that the youngest daughter was laughing and having fun in her section of weeds. The family thought she must be nuts to be able to find joy in such a tedious task. They asked her, "How can you possibly be enjoying this?" She said, "I just imagine I'm picking flowers!"

Stop and smell those flowers. Even if the world is falling apart around us, we can choose to be happy anyway. Focus on those things that bring a smile to your face and try to include them in your daily life. I have a list of happy things that I call my "Elevating Attitude Shifters." Whenever I am discouraged, I look at that list and focus on all of the things I'm grateful for. When life isn't what you hoped it would be, you can still find happiness in it. Happiness is a choice.

So, why doesn't the world just repent already? There's that thing called agency. The Lord isn't going to drag us kicking and screaming into the celestial kingdom. Everyone gets to choose where they want to live for eternity. Life is choices. Every day you choose which side you're on by what you do, how you act, what you say, and how you treat others.

Have you ever noticed how cheerful our modern-day prophets are? They know things are going to get hairy before the Savior's Second Coming, yet they focus on the miracles and amazing things that will also happen in the future. When President Gordon B. Hinckley was aging, his doctor told him he needed to be careful walking, so he gave the prophet a cane to carry. President Hinckley literally carried it and used it as a poker and pointer, rather than as an aid for walking. He even used it to resemble a sword and dubbed Elder Eyring a pretend knight with it. I love how President Hinckley always had a bright smile, even when the world was turning dark around us. I think it was because he knew how the story is going to end (hint: God wins!).

Jenkin Lloyd Jones wisely pointed out, "Anyone who imagines that bliss is normal is going to waste a lot of time running around shouting that he's been robbed. The fact is that most putts don't drop, most beef is tough, most children grow up to just be people, most successful marriages require a high degree of mutual toleration, most jobs are more dull than otherwise. The trick is to thank the Lord for letting you have the ride."[26]

Before I left on my mission, I read a fantastic book called *Man's Search for Meaning* by Viktor Frankl, a Jewish Holocaust survivor who was in a concentration camp during World War II. Frankl watched his fellow prisoners wither and die as everything was stripped from them: their families, their home, their jobs, their world. He saw many of them sink into despair and give up all hope. He realized that you can have everything taken away from you, except one thing: your choice to be happy. No one can force you to be unhappy. You get to decide.

He also learned a profound truth: When you forgive, you don't change the past; you change the future. Years later, he stood face to face with one of the Nazi soldiers who had tormented him. He had to decide if he would let anger and bitterness swallow him up or if he would release those poisons from him and focus on his bright future. He chose to focus on what *could* be, rather than what *was*. That is so powerful.

Never give up hope. If you think life is never going to get better, you're wrong. Hope is a very powerful thing. Sometimes it's all you're hanging on to. Keep holding on. I promise it's going to get better.

Now, if you think your life is simply too hard for you to be happy, allow me to introduce you to someone I know.

Throughout his life, Jesus encountered numerous challenges:

- **Despised Minority:** As a Jew under Roman rule, He belonged to a marginalized group.
- **Oppressive Taxes:** The Roman taxation system burdened the populace.
- **Uncertain Survival:** Living in a time of political unrest, stability was precarious.
- **Restrictive Religion:** Religious practices were stringent and often devoid of joy.
- **Humble Origins:** Nazareth was a town with a questionable reputation.
- **Uneducated Followers:** His disciples were often seen as unrefined.
- **Personal Betrayals:** He faced ingratitude and betrayal from close associates.
- **Violent Death:** Ultimately, he was subjected to a brutal crucifixion.

Do we have faith and trust to put our life and happiness into His hands? Every time we suffer, we are on trial. Will we be obedient and submissive to God's will? God's honor is also on trial. We believe *in* Jesus, but do we believe *Him*?

Throughout His ministry, Jesus exemplified a unique approach to life's challenges:

- **Healing:** He viewed sickness as an opportunity to demonstrate compassion and restore health.
- **Forgiveness:** He saw personal abuses and offenses as chances to teach and practice forgiveness.
- **Empowerment:** Instead of being overwhelmed by societal issues, He was inspired to act, envisioning a transformed world.

Magdala: A Special Place To Honor Women of the Bible

There isn't much to see at station 8, but please allow me to take a quick indulgent tangent and tell you about a fantastic place to visit that honors the women in the New Testament of the Bible, especially those who knew Jesus. Go to Magdala! It's about a two-hour drive from Jerusalem and is well worth your time, especially if you're a woman.

There is a beautiful new hotel there right on the Sea of Galilee, where you can see people getting baptized almost every day. It has such a peaceful, gentle spirit about it. It's a lovely place to visit, but try to stay there if you can so that you have time to bask in the glow of the sunrises and sunsets.

The Magdala Hotel is the perfect place to stay while you take day trips to other important New Testament sites nearby. Plus, their

breakfast and evening buffets are absolutely fantastic. It's a bit pricey but definitely worth it and may be one of the highlights of your trip to Israel.

The Sea of Galilee is the lowest freshwater lake in the world. Heavenly Father loves to make a point through symbols. It's no coincidence that Jesus served in an area considered to be lowly, showing that He "descended below all men" (Doctrine and Covenants 122:8). The Sea of Galilee is mentioned or alluded to more than forty times in the scriptures, being called Tiberias, Gennesaret, a lake, or a sea.

It's not just a picturesque body of water; it's a symbol of faith, trust, and the remarkable power of hope. From Jesus walking on its waters to the miracles He performed on its shores, the Sea of Galilee embodies the profound connection between humanity and the divine.

On the hotel site is a re-created synagogue called The Encounter Room, which has been dedicated to the women in Jesus's life. The stones used in the room are taken from excavation sites nearby. The chapel was built to commemorate the importance of women in the life of Jesus. A gorgeous painting memorializes the moment the woman with the issue of blood touched the hem of Jesus's garment (Luke 8:43–48; Mark 5:22–26). That event didn't happen here, but the beautiful painting of it will capture your heart. (And there are two gift shops on site where you can purchase various sizes of this breathtaking painting.)

The scriptures tell us that after years of spending time, money, hope, and pain to find something that would heal her medical issue without success, the woman with the issue of blood reached to the Savior for help. The Mosaic law had declared her unclean, so she risked punishment or even death if she had been seen in the crowd of people who swarmed around Jesus. She decided to go to Jesus anyway. Do we make the intentional decision every day to seek Jesus in our own lives? He took this woman from a dark place to a place of healing, and He can do that for us too.

Magdala symbolizes transformation and redemption, also shown in the incredible journey of Mary Magdalene in the New Testament (Luke 8:1–3; Matthew 27:55–56). From being possessed by demons to becoming one of Jesus's most loyal disciples, Mary Magdalene's story speaks of the power of faith, renewal, and the capacity for personal transformation. Just being in Magdala can ignite a sense of hope and

possibility, reminding us that no matter where we come from, we have the potential for profound change.

Outside that chapel is an indoor rotunda with columns etched with the names of many faithful women from scripture. The pillars in the atrium represent different women who supported the Savior's ministry like those found in Luke 8:2–3, Matthew 27:56, Luke 23:49 and 55, and Luke 24:10. One pillar is left blank to represent all of the women who enter the church and support Christ in His ministry. Be sure to take a picture of you spiritually standing with Christ and these faithful women next to the blank column.

One night when I was staying at this hotel, I was walking back to my room when I saw a group of Catholic nuns leaving another chapel on site, laughing and standing close to each other in warm friendship. They seemed to be really enjoying each other's company. It felt like such a celebration of sisterhood. This place in Magdala is filled with it.

There is such a celebration of faith in Israel. People boldly wear their faith in their clothing and expressions of worship. I absolutely love it.

Next to that modern rotunda is a beautiful chapel with breathtaking views of the Sea of Galilee and a replica of a first century fishing boat. There are so many special areas on this property where you can quietly reflect on the life of Jesus. It is truly special.

One of the remarkable features of Magdala is the ongoing preservation and excavation efforts that have unveiled a treasure trove

of historical and archaeological wonders. You get to walk through the remains of a first century synagogue, complete with beautifully intricate mosaics and ritual baths. These discoveries offer a glimpse into the religious and cultural practices of the time, providing a tangible connection to the ancient world. It's truly awe-inspiring to witness the preservation of Magdala's rich heritage and the dedication of experts who continue to unravel its mysteries.

During construction of the hotel grounds in 2009, workers uncovered ancient ruins of one of only seven known synagogues from the first century to exist today, dated to around Jesus's time. They stopped construction for a time in order to properly excavate the site, which visiting tourists get to see now. The best preserved synagogue leads scholars to believe Christ visited this very spot (Mark 1:39; Matthew 15:39).

As you wander through the archaeological site, you'll come across remnants of an ancient marketplace and a harbor. Just imagine the bustling activity that once took place there, with merchants selling their wares and fishermen preparing for their voyages on the shimmering Sea of Galilee. After thousands of years, it's truly mind-blowing that new fragments of history are just now being uncovered.

One of the most amazing discoveries during the excavation of the grounds was what they now call the Magdala Stone, which looks like a

box carved out of quartzite stone. On it, you can see a carving of a traditional seven–branched Jewish menorah, making it the oldest carved image of the Second Temple ever found in a public place. Because the menorah is seated on a tripod

base, it is believed that the artist who carved the stone must have seen it in the temple. Other images of the temple are also on the Magdala Stone. The stone box was found almost in the center of the uncovered synagogue area, leading further thought that it might have been used in the Jewish religious service to hold the Torah.

And what about the name Magdala? In Hebrew, it means "tower" or "fortress." It perfectly captures the defensive nature of this ancient settlement, standing tall against the tests of time. In Greek, Magdala is called Taricheae, which means "fish salting," referring to the active commercial fishing that occurred there anciently as well as today. Just down the street from the Magdala Hotel is a popular fish restaurant where you can eat fish from the Sea of Galilee.

Magdala has a sweet symbol that can be seen all over the grounds of the Hotel Magdala and in the city: a six-petaled flower that especially appeals to women. It was found on the Magdala Stone where the menorah was also carved. The rosette is a common Jewish motif found on tombs from the Second Temple period as well. Jewish scholars have a theory that it represents passing through the veil of this life into the presence

of God. You can purchase it on necklaces, t-shirts, rings, and so on.

Continuing on the Via Dolorosa Route

To continue to the next station on the Via Dolorosa, keep walking down this street (Aqabat Al-Khanqah) and turn right at the dead end. The Souq Khan al-Zeit is one of the busiest and most historically significant markets in the Old City of Jerusalem, especially in the Christian Quarter where you are now. Walk for a few minutes on Souq Khan Al Zeit Street until you see some stairs leading outside to the right. You will see a big metal door (most likely it's still painted blue) which remains closed and used to be the original entrance to the Church of the Holy Sepulchre.

You can't get there that way anymore, so climb up the stairs to the left of that metal door, winding around outside in the sunshine. You might notice the Russian symbol and writing on a building, which is owned by the Russian Orthodox church, just east of the Church of the Holy Sepulchre. Keep going and you'll pass another building owned by the Coptic church (the Christians of Egypt), a sect that began in the third century. They have their own liturgy and have preserved old hieroglyphics from centuries past.

While you continue to climb up the stairs, you'll get a peek at the two famous domes on the top of the Church of the Holy Sepulchre. The smaller dome is right over the hill of crucifixion, believed to be Golgotha. The larger dome is over the traditional site of the tomb of Jesus where He was buried and resurrected.

Go through a short tunnel. After a few minutes, you'll arrive at station 9 on the right side where you will see the marker. This is the last station outside the Church of the Holy Sepulchre.

Related Scriptures

Luke 23:27–31

- As Jesus is led to His crucifixion, a large crowd of people, including women, mourns for Him. Jesus responds by telling

them not to weep for Him, but for themselves and their children, as difficult times are coming.

- He prophesies that people will wish for a time when they were barren, and in despair, will call for the mountains and hills to fall on them.
- He warns that if such suffering happens while He, the "green tree," is still alive, even greater suffering will come when He is gone, symbolized by the "dry tree."

Bring This Station to Life

Several talks during the October 2024 general conference reminded us to look for opportunities to share the gospel with others. I know, the prophet and apostles remind us to do missionary work at every general conference, but there was an urgency to their messages this time. Did you feel it?

The world needs more joy, and we have it! The gospel of Jesus Christ is the good news we can tell others about. As a family, make a list of people you know who you could invite over for dinner or to church. I know this can be scary, but the joy we share comes back an hundred-fold.

I had the great privilege of serving a full-time mission in Spain. It was incredibly hard but wonderful and life changing. In one area, I served with a group of truly outstanding missionaries. We got a kick out of each other, worked really hard, and loved spending time with each other. One morning, the eight of us missionaries who were serving in the same little town gathered to hold our weekly district meeting at the church. We took turns organizing our efforts, sharing spiritual messages, bearing testimony to one another, and getting reenergized to go out and find souls to bring to Christ.

We were pretty pumped up and walked out of the church building together, feeling on fire to work hard again. As we walked down the street, one of the missionaries pointed at some people nearby who were oblivious to this powerful team of missionaries in their presence. He proudly proclaimed, "If they really knew who we were, they would come running to us!" Feeling like God's powerful army, the rest of us agreed and patted ourselves on the back for being the Lord's mighty representatives on earth. We whooped and cheered about how great it was to be a missionary and how we were going to baptize the entire country.

Finally, our district leader quietly corrected us with love. He humbly said, "No, you've got it backwards. If we really understood who *they* were, we would be running to them." The group instantly became silent. The truth cut us to our core. He was right. I'll never forget that moment. It brings tears to my eyes even now. Our duty, our calling, our privilege is to help our dear brothers and sisters come unto Christ. It is an honor to be a part of the Lord's great work. Now, let's get to it!

Suggested Hymns to Sing as a Family

7: The Morning Breaks
309: As Sisters in Zion

CHAPTER 11

STATION 9
Jesus's Third Fall

A sign at the entrance and below a small church identifies the ninth station as the Coptic Orthodox Patriarchate, Jerusalem, St. Antony Coptic Monastery, 325 A.D. Saint Anthony was considered the first Christian monk. Next to this church is another Coptic church named Queen Helen Church Coptic Orthodox. Helena Augusta was the mother of Emperor Constantine and encouraged him to embrace Christianity, which he did. She was fascinated by Jerusalem and desperately wanted to find the true locations where the most significant events of Jesus's life occurred. She was the one who identified and approved the location of the Church of the Holy Sepulchre, the site of stations 10–14 on the Via Dolorosa. In some of the tourist shops in the Old City, you can find replicas of the coin that was made with Helena Augusta's image on it. Coins dating to the mid-first century were found in the ruins of Queen Helena Adiabene's palace in Jerusalem.

Helena Augusta's son, Constantine the Great, became the emperor of Rome when his father died in AD 306. After his conversion to Christianity, he issued the "Edict of Milan" in AD 313, which insisted on religious tolerance to Christians all over the Roman empire, making persecution of them illegal. He also created Constantinople (named after him and now called Istanbul), which became the most powerful city in the world at that time. He also funded the building of Christian churches and printing of copies of the Bible.

Queen Helen also discovered a huge cistern cut into a rock, which was used by the construction workers who built the Church of the Holy Sepulchre in the fourth century to memorialize the crucifixion and burial locations of Jesus Christ. It was said that God provided that cistern, and it was the only source of water needed while the big church was being built. God *did* provide the "living water" that we all need: Jesus Christ!

You can now see that well inside this little church dedicated to Queen Helen by following the signs to "Helen's Cistern" beneath the chapel. (It's truly amazing and humbling that so many signs in Jerusalem are written in English.) Be forewarned: the stone steps are quite steep and narrow. At the bottom of the stairs, you can stand and hear a lovely echo, so many tourists like to sing hymns there.

The ninth station doesn't have biblical evidence. It simply describes the third time Jesus stumbled and fell. He must have been completely exhausted at this point, after being scourged, flogged, beaten, starved of food and water, and forced to carry a heavy cross beam while blood dripped down His head from the crown of thorns brutally placed there by Roman guards.

We don't know if Queen Helen was correct about the locations of these events in Jesus's final hours, but I love her enthusiasm and willingness to do the research. She made a difference. She is even revered as a saint in several Christian traditions. We may not make a huge difference in history like she did, but we can do our best to share the gospel, stand for truth, and bring others to Christ like Queen Helen did.

Whether you want to or not, you influence others—for good or for bad. Here's a simple example. My third son is super social and fun. During his junior year in high school, he decided to declare a "Suit Up

Day" at school and convinced all of his bros to dress up in suits to add some class to the joint.

Latter-day Saint young men are used to wearing suits, but none of my son's non-member friends were. It was kind of a big deal for them to agree to do this. Many of them didn't even own suits, but they loved the idea and wanted to participate, so they made it happen. Needless to say, seeing all of these guys dressed up with suits and ties created quite a stir at school. All of the girls were extremely impressed. It was such a hit that they had a few more "Suit Up" days at that school before he graduated. The bottom line is that people watch you and follow your example. Be sure to show them what a "real" Christian is like.

Being a faithful follower of Jesus Christ brings many blessings, especially when you open your mouth to teach others about Him. Here's an example. Would you be happy if I gave you a free scoop of ice cream? If you're like me, you're yelling, "Yes, please! Now, please!" as you hold out your hands. How about if I offered you a double scoop? Nice, right? Well, if you like that, how would you feel if I presented you with a gigantic hot fudge sundae with several scoops of different flavors of ice cream, yummy toppings, fresh bananas and strawberries on the side, huge piles of whip cream, and a cherry on top? Now, all you ice cream haters, be quiet . . . let me make my point. A scoop is great, right? Two scoops make you do the happy dance! But a big sundae is just plain awesome.

Allow me to share with you an example I experienced that illustrates true joy in living the gospel and letting your light shine. When I was in high school, my boyfriend joined the Church. What a wonderful scoop of ice cream! It was awesome and delicious to my soul. It was an amazing experience to go through the missionary discussions with him, sit next to him in seminary and church, discover answers to both of our questions, and grow spiritually together. Delicious ice cream. Incomprehensible joy. I highly recommend it!

When my boyfriend turned nineteen, he was called to serve a mission. I was so excited for him and couldn't wait to write to "my" missionary. I was so proud of him, and I discovered an increasing amount of joy in reading about his experiences and watching him deepen his understanding of the gospel and love for the Savior while he served his mission. Pass the double scoop of ice cream! I felt more than happiness; I felt an abiding joy that I knew was eternal.

Now, here comes the good part. When he was almost finished with his mission, I received a very special letter in the mail. It was from a teenager who had been baptized by my boyfriend. He had submitted his own mission papers and just received a call to serve. In the letter, he thanked me for being brave and teaching my boyfriend about the gospel of Jesus Christ when we were teenagers. I cannot even describe the depth of joy I felt to know that my meager missionary efforts with my boyfriend had rippled out to include this stranger who would then go on to teach others. My heart almost burst. That, my dear friend, is a hot fudge sundae.

Continuing on the Via Dolorosa Route

To get to the next station, walk around the corner. You are now on the rooftop of the Church of the Holy Sepulchre. Ethiopian monks live in a monastery inside this church. It's called Dier es-Sultan and was built to provide shelter for Ethiopian pilgrims and monks. It includes ruins of a medieval cloister, paintings of Ethiopian saints, and a cupola that lets light into St. Helena's crypt below.

Unfortunately, it has been so poorly maintained that you'll be surprised anyone could possibly live there. You may actually see Ethiopians hanging around the area. Some Ethiopians believe that the tree among the ruins is the actual location where Abraham was going to sacrifice his son. The dome of the rock nearby on Temple Mount is said by Jews and Muslims to be the true location of that event described in Genesis 22:1–19.

You can go into St. Michael's Ethiopian church in this compound to arrive at the entrance of the Church of the Holy Sepulchre by walking down a series of stairs. You'll think you've gone the wrong way, but keep walking down the steps. It's a secret shortcut that the public is welcome to use.

You will arrive in the courtyard at the front of the Church of the Holy Sepulchre, where there will most likely be a huge crowd and lines to get into the church. If the door to St. Michael's is closed, then you'll need to backtrack to the markets of Souq Khan al-Zeit. From there, turn right onto Souq al-Dabbagha. After about 260 feet, turn right and you will see a small archway with the words "Holy Sepulchre" which leads you into the big courtyard of the Church of the Holy Sepulchre, the location of the last five stations of the Via Dolorosa.

Related Scriptures

This final fall is not mentioned in scriptures, but it is quite probable that Jesus would have stumbled several times on these uneven stones while walking up an incline, soaked in blood, thirsty, humiliated, hungry, wounded, and exhausted.

Bring This Station to Life

With your family, make a list of ways you can play a bigger role in the Christian conversation in the world. See if there is a good interfaith event or organization in your city. For example, I currently live in Las Vegas, where a fantastic interfaith group meets once a month to share their faith and educate each other in a loving, non-confrontational way. They host a special meeting at different religious locations each time and choose a theological topic to discuss, such as marriage, life after death, and so on. They invite six speakers to explain what their religion believes about the designated topic, and then the audience can ask questions. The church that hosts the meeting provides refreshments during the socializing time at the end. I've attended these inspirational events in a Buddhist temple, Jewish synagogue, Latter-day Saint chapel, and Muslim Mosque. It's wonderful!

When I lived in Georgia, I was involved with the American Mother's Inc., an organization that hosted an amazing interfaith breakfast around Mother's Day. We invited leaders from a variety of religions to talk about how they honor motherhood and families.

There is no denying that members of The Church of Jesus Christ of Latter-day Saints have a special glow about them and a twinkle in their eye, so we just need to get out there, rather than hanging out with only other members of the Church. Be bold and brave.

Suggested Hymns to Sing as a Family

108: Lord, I Would Follow Thee
18: Go Ye Therefore

CHAPTER 12

STATION 10
Jesus Is Stripped of His Garments

People on pilgrimage stop in the courtyard outside the entrance of the Church of the Holy Sepulchre to gather in their groups and reflect on what Christ went through for us. Most Christian denominations consider this giant church to be the holiest spot on earth.

You can see people praying, lighting candles, listening to sermons from their religious leaders, learning about history from their tour guides, crying, and sincerely worshipping in many ways. It doesn't look

or feel like our beautiful and bright Latter-day Saint temples; however, many people feel the Spirit of the Lord here. You might too. Simply reflecting on the last excruciating hours of Christ's life while you stand in this holy city will be an incomparable experience.

Because there is so much packed into this church, many tourists simply walk by various things without realizing their significance to the devout Christian pilgrims who come here to worship. In the next few chapters, I'll point out items and locations you definitely don't want to miss in this huge building.

The original building on the site was a pagan temple on a stone quarry built by the Roman emperor Hadrian in AD 135. Later, a shrine was built by the Christian Emperor Constantine between AD 326 and 335, three hundred years after the Savior's crucifixion. There are several compelling reasons this church's location may or may not be the correct site for the events it claims in the Via Dolorosa path; however, it's a fascinating place to visit, worship, and remember how the Lord's last hours unfolded. Don't allow the debates among archeologists to diminish your spiritual experience here.

The shape of the entrance with its columns and arches was completed during a renovation by the Crusaders in 1149. The original church from the Byzantine era was almost four times bigger than what we see today, which is especially impressive to imagine when you see how large this church is. Today's architecture blends Muslim and

Roman elements, as the church has been rebuilt many times over by the people who controlled it over the centuries.

Today, six groups claim authority over the church property or functions: Greek Orthodox, Armenian, Roman Catholic, Ethiopian, Muslim, and the Jewish state of Israel. The groups even argue over who owns a certain stairway. For example, if you see Latin words above an arch, then the Roman Catholic Church has claimed that as theirs. It's a messy, complicated mixture, both politically and religiously, but it works.

Because the Church of the Holy Sepulchre is a major pilgrimage destination and one of the most important sites in all of Christendom, it is heavily guarded by police and CCTV cameras. More than four million spiritual pilgrims visit every year. The busiest times to visit are during Easter and Christmas.

The Church of the Holy Sepulchre is located in the Christian Quarter of the Old Jerusalem city and was built in AD 335. It is huge on the outside and very dark inside, filled with paintings, sculptures, markers, hanging lamps, and thick incense—a true sensory overload. Pilgrims converge around the most important spots. It is crowded, noisy, overwhelming, and spiritually powerful to everyone who enters.

The entire church complex includes services by three different religious groups: the Greek Orthodox Church, the Roman Catholic Church, and the Armenian Church. A few of the chapels are also used by the Coptic Orthodox and Syrian Orthodox Churches. Even more impressive about this unified effort is that a Muslim family is in charge of opening the doors at sunrise and closing them again at sunset. Talk about teamwork!

Now, get ready for something quirky and fascinating: the Immovable Ladder. This wooden ladder has been leaning against the church's facade for centuries, and it can't be moved without a consensus from all the Christian denominations sharing guardianship of the church. It's a physical reminder of the delicate balance and cooperation required to maintain this holy site. You can see the ladder just outside the building's entrance above the arch and below a window. No one knows why it's there, but because a status quo agreement was made in 1757, all of the governing churches of the Church of the Holy Sepulchre have to agree to move it—and none of them have.

The Roman Column

Don't go inside just yet. Notice the Roman column to your right, next to the exterior stairs. Columns were lovely as a decorative element in Jerusalem, but they also served important functions and landmarks. The column below the stairs is said to be the exact spot where Jesus was stripped of His clothes. He was then led up the hill to Golgotha behind that column. Many claim that column is the tenth station, although there is no official marker there like at the other stations. A small Franciscan chapel inside the Church of the Holy Sepulchre called the Chapel of the Apparition also claims to have the exact column where Jesus was scourged and stripped.

Romans desired to punish and crucify their criminals in the most public places possible. This area would have been extremely busy, as crowds would have traveled to Jerusalem for the Passover pilgrimage. Josephus, the Jewish historian and a contemporary with the Gospels' authors, wrote that more than two million people might have been in the Old City at that time. They would have come to purchase lambs to sacrifice at the temple. Remember, the field outside the city walls was where the sheep were kept and sold.

In the Savior's last week of mortal life, He was presented as the Paschal Lamb on Passover Thursday. In Jewish tradition, the Passover lamb was to be chosen on 10 Nissan on the Jewish calendar, on the tenth day of the lunar month (Zechariah 9:9). That is exactly when Jesus rode in on a donkey during His triumphal entry into Jerusalem.

The Passover lamb needed to meet the following requirements to be sacrificed correctly based on Jewish law:

- The lamb must be the firstborn (Exodus 13:2, 12; D&C 93:21).
- The lamb must be a male (Exodus 12:5; Matthew 1:21).
- The lamb must be without blemish (Exodus 12:5; Hebrews 7:26–27; 1 Peter 2:22; Malachi 1:7–14; 3 Nephi 12:48).

- No bones of the lamb were to be broken (Psalm 34:20; Exodus 12:46; John 19:34–36).
- The lamb was to be killed from noon to 3:00 (John 19:14).
- The lamb was to be eaten near the spot of the sacrifice with no flesh carried far away (Exodus 12:8, 46; John 19:41).
- Nothing of it shall remain until the morning (Exodus 12:10).

Jesus *is* the Lamb of God! Don't you just love when God makes the symbols so obvious?

The next four stations represent events on Atoning Friday. Today, Christians call it Good Friday. It was good for us because it led to our redemption; however, it was brutal for Jesus. The best part of the story is what happened on Resurrection Sunday.

The Chapel of the Franks

The exterior stairs lead inside to the Chapel of the Franks. Unfortunately, these stairs are often gated. Visitors used to be able to walk inside the Chapel of the Franks, a Roman Catholic Crusader chapel that was also said to be the official marker of the tenth station of the Via Dolorosa. It's also known as the Chapel of Torment, Chapel of the Seven Sorrows of the Blessed Virgin Mary, or Our Lady of Sorrows. It was built in the twelfth century when it provided exclusive access to Calvary. Today, it features a blue dome, an eighteenth century gilded wooden altar, and a polychromatic floor. If you can't get in, don't worry. You'll be able to peek into it from a window on the inside of the Church of the Holy Sepulchre.

Now it's time to walk into the Church of the Holy Sepulchre. It's a lot to take in. Members of the Church of Jesus Christ may not initially

respond well to the gaudy, dark elements and noise inside the entire church building; it's so opposite from the light, airy, quiet temples we know and love. We have to remember that for these older Christian religions, their desire is to present the most ornate and expensive materials they can to show how much they love God, the king worthy of all our adoration and worldly possessions.

Just like them, The Church of Jesus Christ of Latter-day Saints erects monuments and memorials to commemorate significant events in our church's history. Think of the Moroni monument on the Hill Cumorah in Palmyra, New York, or some of the old sites in Nauvoo, Illinois, or Kirtland, Ohio. Monuments help us give pause to remember important events. Just because others don't worship the same way we do doesn't mean they're not worshipping or that their hearts aren't sincere.

One of the most captivating features of the Church of the Holy Sepulchre is its unique architectural blend. As you wander through its corridors and chambers, you'll notice elements from different historical periods. From the grand Byzantine architecture to the intricate Crusader decorations and the elegant Ottoman additions, the church reflects the diverse influences and styles of the civilizations that have left their imprint on Jerusalem over the centuries.

This isn't a cathedral in the traditional sense but a collection of chapels built over significant sites that commemorate important moments in Christianity. I've heard many members of the Church of Jesus Christ say they can't feel the Spirit in big cathedrals or dark, dingy chapels. If we are trying to live a life worthy of the constant companionship of the Holy Ghost, we should be able to feel the inspiration of the Spirit almost anywhere: in the grocery store, in our car, in a meadow, in a dirty home where we minister to someone in our ward or branch, and even in a building belonging to another religion.

All of these locations along the Via Dolorosa were lovingly designed to worship the Savior by sincere believers who did their best. During my time in Jerusalem, with my focus on Jesus Christ, my brother who redeemed me from all of my sins, I felt the Spirit in these places and often had to fight back the tears that constantly fell down my cheeks. Being in Jerusalem is such a moving experience.

I have always loved the variety of architecture of places of worship from all religions. The soaring spires of gothic Cathedrals throughout Europe elevate my eyes and thoughts to heaven. The gold-encrusted frames that feature religious artwork from the Early Renaissance cause me to imagine the awe and reverence for God that poor peasants must have felt when they gazed upon them. Small cave-like chapels humble my soul when I see how it is truly mankind's desire to know God and worship Him.

Continuing on the Via Dolorosa Route

After you lift your jaw off the floor, quickly turn right and start walking up the small, narrow staircase. Watch your head! The stairs will take you to the eleventh and twelfth stations, which is where many believe Jesus was crucified and died on Golgotha.

At the top of the stairs, you will be in the hallway that leads to the hill of the crucifixion for the next station. Notice how old these tread-worn stairs are. Even more impressive is imagining how many millions of people over the centuries have walked up them with the sole purpose of remembering Jesus on the cross and thanking Him for His infinite Atonement.

Related Scriptures

The stripping of Jesus's garments before His crucifixion is mentioned in all four Gospels of the New Testament.

Matthew 27:28

- They stripped Jesus and put a scarlet robe on Him.

Matthew 27:31

- After that they mocked Jesus, they took off His robe and put His own clothes on Him.
- They led Jesus away to crucify Him.

Mark 15:20 (This account parallels Matthew's version.)

- After they mocked Jesus, they took off the purple robe and put His own clothes back on Him.
- They led Him out to crucify him.

Luke 23:34

- While Luke does not specifically mention the act of stripping, he records this moment Jesus saying, "Father, forgive them; for they know not what they do."
- They parted His raiment, and cast lots. Here, the focus shifts to the soldiers casting lots for Jesus's garments after He was stripped and crucified.

John 19:23–24

- Then the soldiers cast lots for Jesus's clothes. John provides the most detailed account, explaining how the soldiers divided Jesus's clothing and cast lots for His seamless coat. This fulfilled the prophecy in Psalm 22:18: "They part my garments among them, and cast lots upon my vesture."

Bring This Station to Life

Find ways to gather good people of various religions to do good in your community. Don't focus on debating doctrine but on the common ideal of serving God and mankind. Consider starting a clothing drive to donate to the homeless or women's shelters in honor of this station where Jesus's clothes were stripped from Him. If the many faiths represented at the Church of the Holy Sepulchre can get along, so can we!

Suggested Hymns to Sing as a Family

181: Jesus of Nazareth, Savior and King
183: In Remembrance of Thy Suffering

CHAPTER 13

STATION 11
Jesus Is Nailed to the Cross

This dark hallway chapel, called the Greek Calvary Chapel, marks the eleventh station and claims to be the exact location where Jesus was nailed to the cross. From this hallway, you can also look through an interior window on the right to see the tenth station below, the small Chapel of the Franks, where some believe the Savior's clothing was stripped from Him.

You will see beautiful artwork on the ceiling and walls, all maintained by the Roman Catholic Church. The first painting you will pass illustrates the story of when an angel stopped Abraham from sacrificing his son (Genesis 22:11–12). The Roman Catholic Church strongly

believes that this site is the location of that event with Abraham and Isaac. Abraham named that place "Yahweh-yireh," which means "the Lord will provide." God the Father *did* provide a Savior for all of us to escape the eternal consequences of sin through the atoning sacrifice of His Son, Jesus Christ.

I've often reflected on how Abraham must have experienced the same grief as God the Father when asked to sacrifice his son. We now know that the death of Jesus Christ and His atoning sacrifice ended animal sacrifice. The style of Isaac on the cross in the painting is very similar to the painting straight ahead that shows the Savior being sacrificed on the cross.

The Crucifixion

When you look straight ahead, you will see the painting of Jesus being nailed to the cross. Countless paintings and sculptures have been created over the centuries to memorialize that eternally significant moment in time. Not all paintings of that event are doctrinally accurate, however. Most of them show one nail in the palm of each hand, which is correct but not complete. We know that another nail was added to the wrist of each hand to secure Jesus's body on the cross.

Some paintings show one nail going through Jesus's crossed feet, while others show a nail in each foot. Archeological research has revealed that some prisoners' feet were actually straddled on each side of the cross and nailed from the side.

I find it extremely poignant and symbolic that Jesus washed the disciples' feet during the Last Supper. Traditionally, it was the servants who washed the feet of their master and his special guests. Feet have long been a symbol of the path one takes in life. Possibly to ensure His Apostles understood the symbolism of servant leadership, Jesus removed His outer clothing before washing their feet. His call to them was to serve others, knowing that His own feet would soon be nailed on a cross, ending His mortal ministry.

The inhumane process of crucifixion was the ultimate punishment of criminals and was designed to add shame in a very public setting. It included nudity, violence, and gore in an attempt to dissuade onlookers from committing crimes or resisting Roman rule. It was an effective deterrent; however, it also enraged the Jews and created intense hatred for the Romans, which often caused rebellious uprisings, something Barabbas was known to incite.

Josephus explained that Jewish prisoners "were first whipped and then tormented with all sorts of tortures before they died. Then, they were crucified outside the walls of the city. So, the soldiers, out of the wrath and hatred they bore the Jews, nailed those they caught, one after one way, and another after another, to the crosses, by way of jest, when their multitude was so great, that room was wanting for the crosses, and crosses wanting for the bodies."[27]

Some believe that crucifixion was unique to the Romans, but that's not true. Crucifixion was a method of execution primarily used by the Romans during biblical times, but it was influenced by earlier practices. Crucifixion or impaling is thought to have originated in Persia. It was used as a way to execute enemies and criminals, often by impaling them on a stake. Phoenician and Carthaginian civilizations used forms of crucifixion, particularly for punishing military or political enemies. While not as common in Greek culture, crucifixion was practiced in certain cases. It was considered a degrading punishment reserved for slaves and enemies. Some historical records indicate the use of crucifixion or similar methods in Egypt, particularly under Roman control after its annexation. Crucifixion was widely used in regions under Roman influence, especially in areas of rebellion or unrest, to serve as a brutal public deterrent. Its prominence in the New Testament highlights its association with Roman law and governance in Judea during Jesus's time.

It breaks my heart that so many Jews and Romans rejected the Messiah when He was standing right in front of them. The same is true today. I'll never forget a moment on my mission that taught me a profound truth about why some people accept the gospel and others do not.

It was a hot summer day in Spain, and my companion and I were in our little apartment eating lunch. I walked into our bedroom and heard a fluttering sound. I followed the soft pattering to a huge, heavy armoire. I noticed the bedroom window was open to let the breeze in and then saw a tiny bird stuck between the wall and the big piece of furniture. My arm couldn't reach the bird, and I wasn't strong enough to move the armoire by myself.

Trying to think outside the box, I quickly retrieved a long broom and thought that I could nudge the frightened bird up and out to freedom. But whenever the broom handle would get near the bird, the bird would chirp in fear. I quietly tried to explain to my new feathered friend that I wanted to help it. The more I tried, the more frightened the bird became. I recruited the help of my companion, and together we tried to move the heavy furniture away from the wall to give the bird room to escape. We pushed and heaved for ten minutes, trying to assure the bird that we were trying to help it. My companion and I looked at each other suddenly, realizing that this familiar scenario was how we were spending each day of our mission, trying to help others learn of Christ and be free from their sins.

Many people were afraid of us and would slam their doors when we came knocking. Most of them didn't understand that we just wanted to help make their lives better. They didn't know that our efforts were to save them from spiritual bondage. They just couldn't *see*. Nevertheless, we kept trying. Every day we went out into the world and continued to invite people to hear our message. We couldn't be angry with those who rejected our message because they simply didn't understand what we were offering. Our job was to open our mouths and keep trying. I decided that I probably wouldn't convert the entire country of Spain, but I could love and invite. That's what Jesus Christ did on His mission. I could do the same thing.

The bird story has a happy ending. Eventually we were able to push the huge armoire away from the wall enough that the bird was able to quickly fly away. Did it thank us? Of course not. But we didn't get angry for its lack of gratitude. We didn't judge the bird for getting into that predicament in the first place. We just worked and helped to save one little sparrow. Do you know how the Lord feels about sparrows? He created them and is mindful of their needs (Luke 12: 6–7). Matthew 10 says that the Lord knows the very hairs on your head and that you are of even more value to Him than His precious sparrows. You are His family.

So it is with the world. There will be many who reject the prophets and even you. That's okay. They have their agency to choose. Your job as one of Christ's followers is to keep loving and continue inviting others until you find the ones who are sincerely seeking truth and light. Just keep standing in holy places, and when the Lord comes again, you'll be ready.

It is noteworthy that the Romans did not have to nail someone to a cross in order to crucify them. Sometimes, the Romans simply tied a prisoner to a tree. They quickly realized that having a criminal stretch out their hands was especially excruciating and accelerated death. Some scholars believe this discovery was the reason for the cross to be designed in the shape it was.

Elder Jeffrey Holland stated, "It is one of the most powerful paradoxes of the Crucifixion that the arms of the Savior were stretched wide open and then nailed there, unwittingly but accurately portraying that every man, woman, and child in the entire human family is not only welcome but invited into His redeeming, exalting embrace."[28]

John Flavel, an English Puritan Presbyterian minister and author, quipped, "The scriptures teach us the best way of living, the noblest way of suffering, and the most comfortable way of dying."[29] Jesus showed us how to live correctly, and by dying, He destroyed death!

As members of The Church of Jesus Christ of Latter-day Saints, when we think about the Atonement, we consider what happened on the cross but also what occurred in the Garden of Gethsemane. Please read chapter 17 where I tell you about the Garden of Gethsemane on the Mount of Olives to provide delicious details to enrich your understanding of the complete process of the Atonement, which required both physical and spiritual sacrifice.

Continuing on the Via Dolorosa Route

You will notice fresh flowers and lit candles in this upstairs area, all brought in by sweet visitors who want to show thanks to God and offer their prayers of sincere gratitude. Stay in the chapel area, but walk to your left and you will see station 12.

Related Scriptures

While the Gospel accounts do not explicitly mention nails during the crucifixion narrative, other parts of the New Testament provide this detail:

John 20:25

- After Jesus's resurrection, Thomas mentions the marks of the nails: "The other disciples therefore said unto him, We have seen the Lord. But he said unto them, Except I shall see in his hands the print of the nails, and put my finger into the print of the nails, and thrust my hand into his side, I will not believe."

John 20:27

- Jesus invites Thomas to touch His wounds: "Then saith he to Thomas, Reach hither thy finger, and behold my hands; and reach hither thy hand, and thrust it into my side: and be not faithless, but believing."

Bring This Station to Life

President Russell M. Nelson recently challenged us to read every verse in the scriptures about Jesus. The "Learn of Me" app will walk you through this hefty challenge. This app is designed to facilitate a comprehensive study of the Savior, Jesus Christ, by compiling His words and teachings from the scriptures. It organizes these teachings as found in the Topical Guide from the standard works, providing a structured approach to understanding His life and messages.

Suggested Hymns to Sing as a Family

182: We'll Sing All Hail to Jesus' Name
179: Again, Our Redeeming Lord

CHAPTER 14

STATION 12
Crucifixion and Death

You will see a large sculpture of Jesus hanging and dying on the cross, surrounded by gold, silver, and sculptures of angels dressed in silver gowns and silver halos. Many Christians believe this is the actual spot where Jesus took His last breath and died on the cross; however, there is another location in Jerusalem that is hotly debated as the true location, which we'll talk about later.

On the floor below a Greek Orthodox altar, you can see a fairly large decorated silver disc with a hole that claims to be where the cross beam was set in the rock at Calvary. It is said that if you put your hand in the hole, you are literally touching the site of the cross where Jesus died. During Emperor Constantine's reign, this station was marked with a wooden cross. In AD 417, Emperor Theodosius II replaced it with another cross made of gold and precious stones. Today, it is just a decorated hole. On both sides of the altar are black marble

plates, marking locations of the crosses of the robbers crucified to the left and right of Jesus.

In addition to the hole in the ground, you can see the bedrock this church was built on. Walk around the altar to see the actual rock of Golgotha on the left of the altar on the floor. At the time of Jesus, this location was a rock quarry, and the Church of the Holy Sepulchre was chiseled into it. Under glass, you can see what many believe was the rock of Golgotha, illustrating that it is, indeed, on a hill. It shows a split in the stone that links it to the Christian tradition and scripture about an earthquake occurring when Jesus died (Matthew 27:51).

To the left of the statue of Jesus hanging on the cross is a Latin altar with a bust of Mary, also known as Our Lady of Sorrows, offered to the Church of the Holy Sepulchre by Portugal in 1778. There are additional sculptures and paintings that depict this heartbreaking event in this upper level. Tradition says that the shrine to Mary stands on the very spot where Mary, the mother of Jesus, watched her precious son give His life for all of us on the cross. The sculpture has a sword piercing the heart of Mary. On certain lists, the wooden statue of Mary is the thirteenth station; however, it is not the most popular or common list used today. You also won't see markers for these Via Dolorosa stations inside the Church of the Holy Sepulchre like you did outside on the streets.

All of these events occurred on Friday and were finally completed when Jesus declared it Himself, saying, "Tetelestai," which means "It is finished" in Greek (John 19:30). Have you ever noticed that His sentence was spoken in the present tense? He is indicating that the action has been completed in the past, but it continues into the present. In the Roman Empire, "tetelestai" was written on receipts to show that a purchase had been completed. The price had been paid. It was also used on tax receipts to indicate that a debt had been paid. Let that sink in.

In a judicial context, "tetelestai" means fully served. In a military context, it means "battle won." Jesus truly was the ultimate victor that day. God knows and loves you. John 15:13 states, "Greater love hath no man than this, that a man lay down his life for his friends." That's what Jesus Christ did for you. Elder Jeffrey R. Holland stated, "Trumpeted from the summit of Calvary is the truth that we will never be left alone nor unaided, even if sometimes we may feel that we are."[30]

I know that we can often feel as if God is too busy helping others to know, love, or help us. It's not true. He always knows your situation and can see the long-term plan for what is best for your eternal growth. He knows our hearts and is there to listen, as well as forgive us when we mess up. He knows we're going to mess up. That's why a Savior was provided for us.

When I traveled to Israel, a man in my tour group had served as mission president in Taiwan. He shared a story about how God is exceedingly aware of the details in our lives. He explained that he was super busy one week and didn't have time to answer all two hundred of the weekly emails he received from his missionaries, something that was very important to him. He was busy getting ready for transfers, meeting new missionaries, and fulfilling many other responsibilities.

The week after that, he finally had time to finish reading and replying to the missionaries' letters when he found an email from a sister missionary who said she had found some Spanish-speaking people in her area who desperately needed some Spanish-speaking missionaries. The mission president's heart sank. He felt like he had let down the Lord. He looked at the missionary photo board to see who he had put in that area. He was shocked when he realized that he had sent the only two Spanish-speaking missionaries in the entire mission to that area without even knowing it. The Lord will always make sure important things happen that need to be done to move His work forward.

God is in the details of our lives because He loves us and wants the best for us. One of the Hebrew words for love is "hesed." Hesed is not just a feeling but an action. It "intervenes on behalf of loved ones and comes to their rescue," explained Jewish author Lois Tverberg.[31] Hesed is one of the most fundamental characteristics of God. Bible scholar Darrell L. Bock adds that the word *hesed* is "wrapping up in itself all the positive attributes of God: love, covenant faithfulness, mercy, grace, kindness, loyalty—in short, acts of devotion and loving kindness that go beyond the requirements of duty."[32]

Jesus's sacrifice for us is the ultimate example of hesed. King David wrote about Jesus's death and resurrection in Psalm 22 centuries before those events took place. As a Jew, Jesus knew those scriptures. He had probably memorized them as a young boy. As He began His mortal mission, He also knew those verses were about Him, and He lived His life in submission to His Father.

The Gospel writers each took a unique approach when describing the life of Jesus. Matthew and Mark focused on the human or physical nature of the Savior, while Luke showed few mortal limitations. John avoided the painful reality of how much Jesus suffered in Gethsemane but shared the underlying theology of Jesus's "at-one-ment."

Words to describe "atonement" in various languages add additional insight to our understanding:

- **Hebrew:** kaphar (to cover, wrap, to forgive)
- **Arabic:** kafara (tight squeeze, to draw a thing close)
- **Egyptian:** hapt (ritual embrace)
- **Latin:** capto (robe and hood embracing the body)
- **Aramaic:** kafat (close embrace)
- **Persian:** kaftan (a garment to embrace the body)

The fact that Jesus was crucified between criminals is important. In those days of Roman law, the person who was crucified in the middle was seen as the greater offender. Even in the mocking of Jesus, this moment on the cross displayed the greatest act of love ever known in the history of the world. You could even say that the two arms of Jesus, outstretched, represented the justice of God on the one hand and the mercy of God on the other, coming together in the body of the Savior's sacrifice. How beautiful is that? The crucifixion of Jesus Christ was the ultimate act of selflessness.

Have you felt the Savior's personal, warm embrace as we have walked the Via Dolorosa with Him? He did everything for *you*.

Continuing on the Via Dolorosa Route

To see the final two stations of the Via Dolorosa, keep moving in the room to see touching artwork and to admire the views from this elevated space. Then walk downstairs to the main floor of the street level of the church to station 13.

Related Scriptures

Matthew 27:45–50

- **Verse 50**: "Jesus, when he had cried again with a loud voice, yielded up the ghost."

Mark 15:33–37

- **Verse 37**: "And Jesus cried with a loud voice and gave up the ghost."

Luke 23:44–46

- **Verse 46**: "And when Jesus had cried with a loud voice, he said, Father, into thy hands I commend my spirit: and having said thus, he gave up the ghost."

John 19:28–30

- **Verse 30**: "When Jesus therefore had received the vinegar, he said, It is finished: and he bowed his head, and gave up the ghost."

References to Jesus's Death in Other Parts of the New Testament

Acts 2:23

- "Him, being delivered by the determinate counsel and foreknowledge of God, ye have taken, and by wicked hands have crucified and slain."

Acts 4:10

- "Be it known unto you all, and to all the people of Israel, that by the name of Jesus Christ of Nazareth, whom ye crucified, whom God raised from the dead, even by him doth this man stand here before you whole."

Romans 5:6–8

- "For when we were yet without strength, in due time Christ died for the ungodly."

1 Corinthians 15:3

- "For I delivered unto you first of all that which I also received, how that Christ died for our sins according to the scriptures."

Galatians 3:13

- "Christ hath redeemed us from the curse of the law, being made a curse for us: for it is written, Cursed is every one that hangeth on a tree."

Philippians 2:8

- "And being found in fashion as a man, he humbled himself, and became obedient unto death, even the death of the cross."

Hebrews 2:9

- "But we see Jesus, who was made a little lower than the angels for the suffering of death, crowned with glory and honour; that he by the grace of God should taste death for every man."

1 Peter 3:18

- "For Christ also hath once suffered for sins, the just for the unjust, that he might bring us to God, being put to death in the flesh, but quickened by the Spirit."

Prophetic References to His Death

Isaiah 53:5–6 (Prophecy of the Suffering Servant)

- "But he was wounded for our transgressions, he was bruised for our iniquities: the chastisement of our peace was upon him; and with his stripes we are healed."

Psalm 22:16

- "For dogs have compassed me: the assembly of the wicked have inclosed me: they pierced my hands and my feet."

Bring This Station to Life

Study the seven statements that Jesus made from the cross. These statements are profound expressions of forgiveness, fulfillment of prophecy, care, anguish, and trust. How do these thoughts apply to you? Are you working hard to develop these Christlike qualities?

- **Forgiveness:** "Father, forgive them, for they do not know what they do" (Luke 23:34).
- **Salvation:** "Truly, I say to you, today you will be with me in paradise" (Luke 23:43).
- **Care for His Mother:** "Woman, here is your son," and to the disciple, "Here is your mother" (John 19:26–27).
- **Abandonment:** "My God, my God, why have you forsaken me?" (Matthew 27:46; Mark 15:34).
- **Physical Suffering:** "I am thirsty" (John 19:28).
- **Completion:** "It is finished" (John 19:30).
- **Commitment to the Father:** "Father, into your hands I commit my spirit" (Luke 23:46).

Suggested Hymns to Sing as a Family

192: He Died! The Great Redeemer Died
190: In Memory of the Crucified

CHAPTER 15

STATION 13
Jesus Is Taken Down from the Cross

The thirteenth station is on the main floor at the street level of the Church of the Holy Sepulchre and can be seen when you first walk into the building. The station commemorates Jesus's mortal body being taken down from the cross to be prepared for burial. It causes us to reflect on the Savior's grieving mother, Mary, as she takes His body in her arms. Countless sculptures and paintings have been created over centuries to memorialize this moment. Jesus's body was then laid on the Stone of the Anointment and anointed with a mixture of myrrh and oils.

On the floor of the Church of the Holy Sepulchre is a large piece of stone, called the Stone of Unction, where Jesus's body was said to be carefully prepared for burial, as the Sabbath was quickly approaching. It's common to see people touch it and bend down to kiss the spot to thank the Savior for what He did for all of us. Religious pilgrims can also be seen rubbing oil on the stone with their personal crosses, holy cards, or kerchiefs to take home as a special memento. The stone is not the original slab and dates back to only 1810, but seeing it is impressive because it elicits genuine devotion and worship among its visitors. Tradition says that this stone slab was placed over the original anointing stone that was used to prepare the body of Jesus.

Above the Stone of Unction is a large Greek mosaic that shows the body of Jesus at the Anointing Stone. It is extremely new compared to everything else inside this gigantic church; it was created in 1990. The mural shows three events from the timeline that Friday afternoon: Jesus being taken down from the cross, His body being prepared for burial, and Jesus being taken to the burial cave of Joseph of Arimathea. From the Stone of Unction, the friends and family of Jesus would have looked up on the hill to see Jesus on the cross. All of these sacred sites are said to be located inside the Church of the Holy Sepulchre.

Notice the small basket where the Savior's loved ones placed the nails that were removed from His hands and feet. Can you imagine the tears that flowed and hearts that broke in those moments? Can you imagine how heart-wrenching it must have been for them to wrap the final piece of linen over the Savior's face, assuming they would never see Him again in this life? They still couldn't conceive of the idea that the resurrection Jesus talked about would really happen. No one had ever broken the bands of death before.

In 2016, a conservation team from the National Technical University of Athens uncovered a limestone burial slab inside the tomb of Jesus that had been covered by layers of marble since 1555. Another recent discovery was made in 2024 when archaeologists discovered a long-lost altar at the tomb. Construction work is always going on all over Jerusalem, including at the Church of the Holy Sepulchre.

Recently, a large stone slab covered in graffiti was found leaning against a random wall inside the church. The decorative markings of ribbons on the five-by-eight-food slab convinced researchers it was the Medieval altar over the tomb consecrated in 1149. They thought it had been destroyed in the 1808 fire. Everyone was in awe that it had been hidden in plain site for centuries. Christian tradition states that Christ's body was laid on a slab cut from a limestone cave. Some believe this could be that very slab.

To the left of the Stone of Anointing is a small circular slab with four pillars and a marble canopy. It is called the Station of the Holy Women, although it is not officially one of the Via Dolorosa stations. The Armenian shrine honors Jesus's mother and Mary's companions who viewed the crucifixion, possibly from the very spot it marks. Behind the shrine is a large mosaic that illustrates that moment.

Sacred Oils: Frankincense and Myrrh

The scriptures teach us that special spices and oils were used on Jesus's body. John 19:40 quantified the amount as "an hundred-pound weight," which is only about twelve ounces by US measurement. We know that frankincense and myrrh were given to Mary by the wise men from the East and that they were selected especially for their symbolism to kingship theology. Frankincense was added to a sacred anointing oil blend, which also included myrrh, used only in the temple. Frankincense was also used as an accompaniment to the meat offering, which was part of all burnt and peace offerings in the temple (Leviticus 2:1, 16).

When burned, frankincense symbolized prayer rising to the heavens like smoke, presented to the baby Jesus to represent His later role as a high priest. We pray to God the Father in the name of Jesus Christ, represented by frankincense. For thousands of years, frankincense has been used in religious and spiritual rituals as a symbol of holiness and righteousness. It was used as a religious offering, much like Christ's ultimate sacrifice. Simply put, frankincense represents Jesus's deity. When the wise men from the East brought frankincense to honor Jesus, they were acknowledging that He was no ordinary man but actual Deity. Every earthly king in the ancient world and even Charles II of England today was anointed with oil before being coronated a king.

Myrrh is a sappy resin secreted from the Kamaphora Mura tree. When the tree is wounded, it bleeds and secretes resin we call myrrh. There is powerful symbolic imagery that should immediately cause us to reflect on the crucifixion of Jesus Christ. The word *Mura* (the name of the tree myrrh comes from) is Hebrew and Arabic, and means "bitterness."

When myrrh is soaked in oil, it produces a reddish-brown color similar to the color of blood. The myrrh tree has been considered sacred with its oil intended to heal both physical and spiritual wounds. It is an excellent symbol of Christ because He was in the center of the Garden of Eden, represented by a tree. When you go to the temple, can you think of anything specific that you see or wear that represents that tree? Do you think it's possible that the wise men who brought myrrh to honor the Christ child knew all of this? Absolutely! The use of Mashku oil (myrrh) for anointing kings was a long-standing practice in Mesopotamia. They believed this special oil imbued the king with divine power and legitimacy.

Despite the incredible symbolism God left for the Jews to recognize Jesus as their long-awaited Messiah, many non-believers over the centuries have claimed that Jesus didn't truly die and, most certainly, wasn't resurrected. Several theories have remained to this day, but they are easily disproven with facts and logic.

Continuing on the Via Dolorosa Route

The tomb, and final station, is just around the corner.

Related Scriptures

Matthew 27:57–60

- When the even was come, there came a rich man of Arimathaea, named Joseph, who also himself was Jesus's disciple: He went to Pilate, and begged the body of Jesus. Then Pilate commanded the body to be delivered. And when Joseph had taken the body, he wrapped it in a clean linen cloth, And laid it in his own new tomb, which he had hewn out in the rock: and he rolled a great stone to the door of the sepulchre, and departed.

Mark 15:42–46

- And now when the even was come, because it was the preparation, that is, the day before the sabbath, Joseph of Arimathaea, an honourable counsellor, which also waited for the kingdom of God, came, and went in boldly unto Pilate, and craved the body of Jesus. And Pilate marvelled if he were already dead: and calling unto him the centurion, he asked him whether he had been any while dead. And when he knew it of the centurion, he gave the body to Joseph. And he bought fine linen, and took him down, and wrapped him in the linen, and laid him in a sepulchre which was hewn out of a rock, and rolled a stone unto the door of the sepulchre."

Luke 23:50–53

- And, behold, there was a man named Joseph, a counsellor; and he was a good man, and a just: (The same had not consented to the counsel and deed of them;) he was of Arimathaea, a city of the Jews: who also himself waited for the kingdom of God. This man went unto Pilate, and begged the body of Jesus. And he took it down, and wrapped it in linen, and laid it in a sepulchre that was hewn in stone, wherein never man before was laid."

John 19:38–42

- And after this Joseph of Arimathaea, being a disciple of Jesus, but secretly for fear of the Jews, besought Pilate that he might take away the body of Jesus: and Pilate gave him leave. He came therefore, and took the body of Jesus. And there came also Nicodemus, which at the first came to Jesus by night, and brought a mixture of myrrh and aloes, about an hundred pound weight. Then took they the body of Jesus, and wound it in linen clothes with the spices, as the manner of the Jews is to bury. Now in the place where he was crucified there was a garden; and in the garden a new sepulchre, wherein was never man yet laid. There laid they Jesus therefore because of the Jews' preparation day; for the sepulchre was nigh at hand.

Bring This Station to Life

I highly recommend you listen to *The Ancient Tradition* podcast that takes you through the ages from the very beginning and shows you where all of today's rich rituals, ceremonies, and symbols came from. I promise your mind will be blown and enlightened. There is so much more to these special oils, spices, and stones.

The podcast's content is advanced, so young children will be bored. For them, consider creating a taste test of various spices to see if they recognize them. You could even invite them to create their own special blend to serve with your dinner tonight.

Suggested Hymns to Sing as a Family

186: Again We Meet Around the Board
184: Upon the Cross of Calvary

CHAPTER 16

STATION 14
Jesus's Body Is Laid in the Tomb

In the middle of a large rotunda known by the Greek name "Anastasis" (Resurrection) is an ornate tomb that you can look inside. It is said to be on the exact spot where Jesus was buried. It's called an "Aedicula," a Greek construction with two separate rooms often called the "little house," built in 1810 after the big fire of 1808. The new structure is thick and solid, designed to withstand big earthquakes like the one that occurred when Jesus died and the next big one that will happen at His Second Coming.

The first small room is called The Chapel of the Angel because it contains the Angel's Stone, which is said to be a fragment of the actual stone that once sealed Jesus's tomb. The second small room is the funeral chamber that holds the tomb where many believe Jesus's body was laid to rest after He died. After you look at the tomb in the small chamber, turn around and you will see a huge rock covered in glass. Tradition asserts it to be part of the original rock from the tomb, showing that the tomb was underground, beneath the rock quarry of Golgotha. Both rooms are extremely dark. So was that grim day of the crucifixion.

Unique Worship Services

The gorgeous dome above the rotunda features a decorated starburst of light that represents Jesus's resurrection from the tomb below. I love this imagery. The Miracle of the Holy Fire is an annual event celebrated on Holy Saturday, the day before Orthodox Easter. Orthodox Christians believe that a celestial fire descends upon the Aedicula, symbolizing the resurrection of Christ and the light of Christ's victory over death. The Greek Orthodox patriarch of Jerusalem enters the tomb, prays, and emerges with candles lit by the Holy Fire. This fire is then distributed to the gathered pilgrims who use it to light their own candles.

Traditionally, the fire is said to be cool to the touch and does not burn, symbolizing the divine nature of the miracle. It's a breathtaking spectacle that draws pilgrims from all corners of the globe, each lighting their own candles to bask in the glow of this special event. After the ceremony, the Holy Fire is distributed to special emissaries to take it to various Orthodox countries, including Greece, Russia, and Serbia,

where it is used to light Paschal candles in local churches. It is a wild, exciting ceremony for believers.

Usually, there is an extremely long line to go inside the tomb structure to see the sacred site for only a few brief seconds. When there aren't large crowds, some small groups partake of the Eucharest (sacrament wafer) when they bring a priest as their tour guide and have time inside the tomb.

As mentioned earlier, three major groups manage the Church of the Holy Sepulchre. They reverently and respectfully hold short church services for people of their religion before inviting them to enter the tomb. Everyone waits patiently in line, something that impressed me greatly.

On the opposite side of the tomb's entrance is a triumphal arch built by the Crusaders, representing how the Savior triumphed over death and sin. It leads to the Catholicon, the basilica's central worship space.

You will see a decorated screen called the "iconostasis," which partially hides the altar from view. Women are not allowed to enter the tiny makeshift chapel, yet that does not prevent them from worshipping. Their faith is admirable and extremely touching. Are we as dedicated to finding places and moments each day to give thanks for our Savior?

While standing in a very long line to get inside the tomb site, I was able to watch a short Armenian worship service behind the tomb entrance. The worshippers' devotion was sincere and sweet. I was impressed at how well the various Christian religions that maintain this spot respectfully and patiently give time to one another to hold short services for the members who want to worship right next to the tomb.

While all these religious sects might worship differently than we do, we have to remember that we're all on the same team. We're all believers in Jesus Christ, who died for us. In a world where there is so much evil and hatred, it's comforting to know that Christians all over the world are trying to focus on the Savior, do good, and be good.

Nearby, you will see a goblet standing on a beautiful marble floor, marking the omphalos (the navel), considered to be the center of the earth. The omphalos stone in the Church of the Holy Sepulchre serves as a profound symbol of the centrality of Christ's passion and resurrection in Christian theology, embodying the belief that this site is the spiritual heart of the world.

More to See Inside the Church of the Holy Sepulchre

Now that you've completed the fourteen official stations, be sure to spend more time exploring this gigantic church. There are more than thirty chapels and worship spaces inside this huge building.

If you walk around the site of the tomb toward the back wall, you'll see a hallway with brown wood walls that lead into a first century Jewish tomb. You can crawl inside the dark cave to see two sections used as tombs for individuals. This area is actually an extremely old Coptic chapel called the Chapel of St. Joseph of Arimathea and St. Nicodemus. The tradition is that both of those men were previously buried there. On Sundays and special feast days, it's furnished so it can be used for Catholic mass.

One way to get to the fascinating sites in the basement is through the Armenian chapel. It has lovely artwork with an interesting element. The Armenians in charge of this little chapel did not allow countries to submit artwork that showed pictures of their national flags to hang in the chapel, so instead, the countries sent pictures designed in the colors of their national flags. Definitely take time to notice the ancient graffiti etched into the darker wall as you walk down those stairs into the lower level. Why is that wall darker? Because tourists are touching it all the time. One wall is from the eleventh century, while the other one on the staircase is from the twelfth century.

The Chapel of Saint Helena

This is also an Armenian chapel called the Chapel of St. Helena, named after Constantine's mother. She is the one who first discovered and claimed the entire site of the Church of the Holy Sepulchre as containing the events represented in the last five stations of the Via Dolorosa. This space is also called the Chapel of St. Gregory because of a painting of him on one of the walls. He was known as Saint Gregory the Illuminator, born around AD 240 in modern-day Armenia.

Gregory was imprisoned for thirteen years in a deep pit by the pagan King Tiridates III, who had persecuted Christians. After his release, Gregory healed the sick king, which resulted in mass conversion of the Armenian people. He is now known as the patron saint of the Armenian Apostolic Church, making the country the first nation to adopt Christianity as its state religion. Today, about 97 percent of the population in Armenia still belongs to that church.

The Chapel of the Finding of the True Cross

Walk down another level of stairs. Venturing deeper into the church below, you'll encounter the Chapel of the Finding of the True Cross, which commemorates the moment when Helena (Queen Helen from station 9), the mother of Emperor Constantine, is believed to have discovered the cross on which Jesus was crucified. This event is commemorated annually on September 14, known as the Feast of the Exaltation of the Holy Cross.

This subterranean Chapel of the Finding of the True Cross is the oldest part of the entire Church of the Holy Sepulchre. It is said to be part of the original basilica Emperor Constantine commissioned to be built in the fourth century. The chapel was constructed in the twelfth century and is adorned with remnants of twelfth-century frescoes, though they have become quite faint over time due to centuries of candle smoke and water damage. The stone walls prove this site was built on a rocky quarry.

The Chapel of Adam

On your way back up from the basement, you'll find the Chapel of Adam. The Roman Catholic Church believes this location to be sacred and the actual site where Adam was "born" through the breath of life. You'll see part of the rock of Golgotha behind glass. A curious element of that piece of the rock is that a part of it is stained red as if blood had dripped on it. Indeed, that's exactly what the Catholics claim. They believe that Jesus was crucified over the very spot where Adam began

his life and that some of the blood that was released from Jesus's side when the solider thrust a sword into His body poured directly over the stone.

Thoughts on the Church of the Holy Sepulchre

Many members of The Church of Jesus Christ of Latter-day Saints may roll their eyes at the bold claims that are associated with these sites, and rightly so, since most of them are still hotly debated by archeologists; however, they are still worth visiting because they give us a unique opportunity to think about the Savior and all that He did for us. You can absolutely feel the Holy Ghost testifying to you of the divinity of Jesus Christ at all of these locations.

We haven't talked about it yet, but there is an entire different school of thought among archeologists that the original Temple Mount was not where everyone claims, but on the southwest side of the city and that Jesus would have been presented to the crowds after His condemnation outside Barclay's Gate near what would have been Robinson's Arch. Southern temple excavations have revealed some compelling evidence. Needless to say, debate continues about the true locations of all the events of Jesus's last few hours. The scope of this book has not been to argue for or against the various sites but to focus on the Savior and what He has done for us through His atoning sacrifice.

Now that you've walked the Via Dolorosa path, you should see the "way of the cross" more clearly. At station 1, Pontius Pilate asked Jesus "What is truth?" (John 18:38) but then walked away before allowing the Savior to answer the question. John 14:6 explains that Jesus clarified who He is quite boldly: "I am the way and the truth and the life. No one comes to the father except through me." He never said, "Live your own truth." He *is* the truth.[33]

In the bustling streets of Jerusalem, the Church of the Holy Sepulchre stands as a beacon of hope, peace, and unity in a region marked by its rich tapestry of religions and cultures. It serves as a testament to the power of faith to bring people together, transcending differences and reminding us of our shared humanity and faith in Jesus Christ, the promised Messiah.

What's missing from the Church of the Holy Sepulchre is a visual celebration of the resurrection of Jesus Christ. All of the artwork, chapels, and memorials focus on the crucifixion of the Savior, a vitally important part of the Atonement; however, it would be nice to complete the story with what happened next. The point is that He rose!

Matthew talked about the "sign of Jonah" in chapter 12, verse 40 and chapter 27, verse 40. The Jews knew well the story of Jonah being in the whale for three days. That was one more clue Heavenly Father was trying to give the Israelites so they would recognize the Messiah when He came and would be resurrected after three days.

The Jews also knew the stories of the temple and how it would be destroyed and rebuilt in three days. Mark 14:58 mentions this "temple" was Jesus Christ in the flesh. Did the Jews recognize these symbols? Some did, but many did not.

The risen Jesus *did* return. He appeared to His disciples and followers twelve times before His final ascension:

- Mary Magdalene (Mark 16:9–11)
- The women at the tomb (Matthew 28:8–10)
- Peter (Luke 24:34)
- The travelers on the road (Mark 16:12–13)
- The disciples without Thomas (Mark 16:14)
- The disciples including Thomas (John 20:26–31)
- The disciples while they fished (John 21:1–14)
- The disciples on the mountain (Matthew 28:16–20)
- The crowd of 500 (1 Corinthians 15:6)
- James (1 Corinthians 15:7)
- Those who were at His ascension (Acts 1:6–9)
- Paul (Acts 9:1–6)

Are we paying attention to the symbols and clues Heavenly Father has been leaving for us about the Savior's Second Coming?

Related Scriptures

Matthew 27:57–60

- "When the even was come, there came a rich man of Arimathaea, named Joseph, who also himself was Jesus's disciple: He went to Pilate, and begged the body of Jesus. Then Pilate commanded the body to be delivered. And when Joseph had taken the body, he wrapped it in a clean linen cloth, And laid it in his own new tomb, which he had hewn out in the rock: and he rolled a great stone to the door of the sepulchre, and departed."

2. Mark 15:42–46

- "And now when the even was come, because it was the preparation, that is, the day before the sabbath, Joseph of Arimathaea, an honourable counsellor, which also waited for the kingdom of God, came, and went in boldly unto Pilate, and craved the body of Jesus. And Pilate marvelled if he were already dead: and calling unto him the centurion, he asked him whether he had been any while dead. And when he knew it of the centurion, he gave the body to Joseph. And he bought fine linen, and took him down, and wrapped him in the linen, and laid him in a sepulchre which was hewn out of a rock, and rolled a stone unto the door of the sepulchre."

Luke 23:50–54

- "And, behold, there was a man named Joseph, a counsellor; and he was a good man, and a just: (The same had not consented to the counsel and deed of them;) he was of Arimathaea, a city of the Jews: who also himself waited for the kingdom of God. This man went unto Pilate, and begged the body of Jesus. And he took it down, and wrapped it in linen, and laid it in a sepulchre that was hewn in stone, wherein never man before was laid. And that day was the preparation, and the sabbath drew on."

John 19:38–42

- "And after this Joseph of Arimathaea, being a disciple of Jesus, but secretly for fear of the Jews, besought Pilate that he might

> take away the body of Jesus: and Pilate gave him leave. He came therefore, and took the body of Jesus. And there came also Nicodemus, which at the first came to Jesus by night, and brought a mixture of myrrh and aloes, about an hundred pound weight. Then took they the body of Jesus, and wound it in linen clothes with the spices, as the manner of the Jews is to bury. Now in the place where he was crucified there was a garden; and in the garden a new sepulchre, wherein was never man yet laid. There laid they Jesus therefore because of the Jews' preparation day; for the sepulchre was nigh at hand."

Bring This Station to Life

The Church of the Holy Sepulchre is so large that it can be hard to wrap your head around the interior's floor plan and layers. I encourage you and your family to look online for floor plans and YouTube videos that help you visualize everything better. There are some fantastic walking tour videos that will help you decide which areas you want to focus on if you travel to Jerusalem and have limited time.

To apply this site to the Latter-day Saint mindset, make a list with your family of all the Latter-day Saint historic sites in the United States you'd like to visit one day. You can find a list and map at https://newsroom.churchofjesuschrist.org/article/map-of-the-churchs-20–plus-historic-sites-in-the-us.

Suggested Hymns to Sing as a Family

199: He is Risen
136: I Know That My Redeemer Lives

CHAPTER 17

Additional Sites Related to the Via Dolorosa

I wish that some of the sites listed below were officially included on the official Via Dolorosa route because they're significant and fascinating to visit. They have a direct relation to the events commemorated in the Via Dolorosa route, so I want to make sure you know about them.

The Garden of Gethsemane

No trip to Jerusalem is complete without a visit to the Garden of Gethsemane. Luke 22:39 tells us that Jesus loved this garden and went there often. That's another reminder that nature can be a healing refuge for us. Volumes have been written about what happened in this beautiful grove. (As you know, God loves to make groves sacred, as evidenced by the Sacred Grove during the First Vision.)

The Garden of Gethsemane, located at the foot of the Mount of Olives in Jerusalem, is one of the most sacred sites in Christianity. Its name, derived from the Aramaic word *Gat Shemanim,* means "oil press," indicating its historical use as an olive grove where oil was extracted.

This serene location is famously associated with the events of Jesus's final hours before His crucifixion, as described in the Gospels of the New Testament. Today, it remains a place of reflection and pilgrimage for Christians around the world.

According to the Gospels of Matthew, Mark, and Luke, the Garden of Gethsemane was the site where Jesus prayed fervently the night before His arrest, just hours before the journey of the Via Dolorosa officially began. In Matthew 26:36–46, Jesus is depicted as deeply distressed, asking His disciples to keep watch while He prays to God. He utters the poignant words, "My soul is overwhelmed with sorrow to the point of death. Stay here and keep watch with me." His heart was breaking.

This moment illustrates the intense emotional and spiritual struggle Jesus faced as He anticipated His crucifixion. He asked His disciples three separate times to stay with Him, explaining He was in agony. That is the only time in the entire Bible we see the word *agony*. The word in Greek (*agonia*) denotes a contest or struggle, often associated with intense physical or emotional pain.

In Luke 22:44, it is said that Jesus prayed with such intensity that "his sweat was like drops of blood falling to the ground," a real-life but rare phenomenon known as hematidrosis, which can occur under extreme stress. This detail underscores the gravity of the sacrifice Jesus was about to make. Despite His anguish, Jesus ultimately submits to God's will, saying, "Father, if you are willing, take this cup from me; yet not my will, but yours be done" (Luke 22:42).

This description of Jesus sweating "blood from every pore" mirrors the account in Luke 22:44 in the Bible, which mentions that Jesus's sweat was like drops of blood falling to the ground during His prayer in Gethsemane. As a physician, Luke was the only Gospel writer to talk about how Jesus sweat drops of blood.

The Garden of Gethsemane is also significant for being the place where Jesus was betrayed by Judas Iscariot and arrested by Roman soldiers. In Matthew 26:47–50, Judas arrives with a large crowd armed with swords and clubs. He betrays Jesus with a kiss, a prearranged signal to identify Him to the authorities. Jesus's calm acceptance of His fate in this moment highlights His unwavering commitment to fulfilling His divine mission.

During Jesus's arrest, Peter draws a sword and strikes the servant of the high priest, cutting off his right ear. Jesus immediately intervenes, instructing His followers to cease violence. He then touches the injured man's ear and heals him. This act of healing is recorded in the Gospel of Luke, which provides the most detailed account of the event, demonstrating both the power and kind mercy of Jesus.

This healing demonstrates Jesus's compassion and His commitment to peace, even in the face of betrayal and impending crucifixion. You would think watching that miracle firsthand would have halted the arrest immediately and resulted in the instant conversion of every observer in that party. Clearly, that didn't happen. It makes me wonder how often I experience miraculous moments in my life yet continue living the way I always do as if nothing happened. It's the pattern

Laman and Lemuel showed us time and again in Book of Mormon accounts.

The Bible doesn't clarify that Christ's atoning sacrifice began in Gethsemane, but the Book of Mormon and Doctrine and Covenants do. One key passage is Mosiah 3:7, where the prophet King Benjamin speaks of the Savior's atoning sacrifice: "And lo, he shall suffer temptations, and pain of body, hunger, thirst, and fatigue, even more than man can suffer, except it be unto death; for behold, blood cometh from every pore, so great shall be his anguish for the wickedness and the abominations of his people."

Another important reference in the Book of Mormon is found in Alma 7:11–13, where Alma the Younger speaks of the Savior's role in taking upon Himself the pains and sins of the world: "And he shall go forth, suffering pains and afflictions and temptations of every kind; and this that the word might be fulfilled which saith he will take upon him the pains and the sicknesses of his people... And he will take upon him death, that he may loose the bands of death which bind his people."

In Doctrine and Covenants 19:16–19, the Savior speaks in the first person about His atoning sacrifice: "For behold, I, God, have suffered these things for all, that they might not suffer if they would repent; But if they would not repent they must suffer even as I; Which suffering caused myself, even God, the greatest of all, to tremble because of pain, and to bleed at every pore, and to suffer both body and spirit—and would that I might not drink the bitter cup, and shrink—Nevertheless, glory be to the Father, and I partook and finished my preparations unto the children of men."

This passage directly references the biblical account of Jesus sweating blood in Gethsemane (Luke 22:44) and adds a deeply personal testimony from the Savior about the magnitude of His suffering. It underscores His willingness to endure immense agony to provide a path for humanity's redemption.

The Doctrine and Covenants consistently emphasizes the Atonement as the central act of Jesus Christ's mission and its role in the plan of salvation. While it does not focus on the geographical location of Gethsemane, it clarifies the spiritual and eternal implications of what transpired there and on the cross. It invites readers to reflect on Christ's sacrifice and to respond by repenting and following Him.

You've probably heard that "atonement" means "at-one-ment" or "at one with God." Jesus literally paid the price so that we could be with Him. The cost was the blood of an eternal being.

The olive trees in the Garden of Gethsemane are believed to be among the oldest in the world, with some studies suggesting they date back over two thousand years. These ancient trees might have witnessed the events of that fateful night. Trees have long been a religious

symbol of the people of Israel. In fact, a tree is a symbol of people, God's people. It's an interesting insight when you reflect that Jesus began his atoning sacrifice for the people in a grove of trees, for people.

The symbolism of the olive trees is profound. Olive oil held great cultural, economic, and spiritual significance in Jerusalem during Jesus's time. Its multifaceted role in daily life, religious practices, and symbolism made it a cornerstone of ancient Mediterranean societies, including the Jewish culture of first century Judea. Olive oil production was a significant industry, and the process of pressing olives in facilities like those at the Garden of Gethsemane (meaning "oil press") was a common practice. Jesus Christ was pressed spiritually and physically in the Garden of Gethsemane.

In Jewish religious practices, olive oil was central to temple rituals. It was used to fuel the menorah, the sacred lampstand in the temple, which was to burn continually as a symbol of God's eternal presence (Exodus 27:20–21). Jesus Christ is central to our Latter-day Saint temples, and we make covenants to always remember Him.

Olive oil was also a primary component of anointing oil, which was used to consecrate priests, kings, and sacred objects (Exodus 30:22–33). It was also commonly used for medicinal purposes, often mixed with herbs to create healing balms. Jesus Christ is the balm that heals our pains.

The act of anointing with olive oil was a powerful symbol of being chosen by God. Kings and prophets were anointed to signify their divine appointment and empowerment by the Holy Spirit. The term "Messiah" or "Christ" means "the Anointed One," linking Jesus directly to this tradition. Olive oil's use in anointing emphasized the sacred and divinely sanctioned nature of leadership and mission.

In ancient Israel, olives were pressed three separate times to extract the needed types of oil. The first press resulted in the best quality oil used exclusively in the temple. The second press resulted in good quality oil used for nourishment. The third, and final, press was used to squeeze the last bits in order to have oil used in lamps. Are you seeing the symbolism here?

Jesus had asked His disciples to stay awake and pray with Him *three* times, alluding to these three presses He would have to endure in this olive grove. He was literally being crushed by the weight of the sins of the world. Like the third and final press of the olives that would produce oil to be used in lamps, Jesus, in that moment, truly became the light of the world.

Gethsemane is a blend of the Hebrew words "Gat" and "Shmanim." "Gat" means winepress, while "Shmanin" means oils, the plural word for "Shemen." These words emphasize the profound suffering Jesus endured as part of His Atonement, which includes both His agony in Gethsemane where he was "pressed" and His suffering on the cross.

One of the tender moments that occurred in the Garden of Gethsemane was when an angel arrived to comfort Jesus. Luke 22:43 reveals, "And there appeared an angel unto him from heaven, strengthening him." The scriptures don't tell us who that angel was. Some assume it was Gabriel, since he had been a part of Jesus's life from the beginning when he appeared to Mary at the Annunciation. I like that sweet idea.

Others believe it was Michael because he was there at the very beginning in the Garden of Eden and wanted to ensure that the Savior which God had promised him would be able to make the required sacrifice to save all mankind from sin.

The popular Christian author Max Lucado shared a compelling insight in his daily devotional online called "Come home, God is calling." He said, "The Bible is the story of two gardens: Eden and Gethsemane. In the first, Adam took a fall. In the second, Jesus took a stand. In the first, God sought Adam. In the second, Jesus sought God. In Eden, Adam hid from God. In Gethsemane, Jesus emerged from the tomb. In Eden, Satan led Adam to a tree that led to his death. From Gethsemane, Jesus went to a tree that led to our life."[34]

Michael absolutely could have been the angel that came to give Jesus strength. As with many things about Jerusalem, we just don't know. No matter who the angel was, the imagery inspires me to be that kind of angel to others who are struggling. My favorite quote is, "We are each of us angels with only one wing, and we can only fly by embracing one another."[35]

Eden represents the beginning of humanity's fall and the loss of innocence, where sin entered the world through disobedience. The Garden of Gethsemane represents the beginning of the redemption process, where Jesus, through His obedience and willingness to suffer,

took on the weight of human sin to restore humanity's relationship with God.

The Church of All Nations

The Church of All Nations, also known as the Basilica of the Agony, now stands adjacent to the Garden of Gethsemane, preserving its sanctity and providing a place for worship and reflection. It is a Roman Catholic Church, completed in 1924, and operated by the Franciscan Custody of the Holy Land. It's worth wandering inside just to see the lovely artwork which utilizes the appropriate motif of the olive trees in the garden.

The events in the Garden of Gethsemane serve as a powerful reminder of Jesus's humanity and divinity. His willingness to endure immense suffering for the redemption of humanity is a cornerstone of Christian theology. Today, the garden continues to inspire believers with its rich spiritual significance and historical depth, offering a tangible connection to the Passion of Christ and the events that triggered the Via Dolorosa.

The view of Jerusalem in the photo above was taken from inside the Garden of Gethsemane. Perfectly framed between two pickets are the

Golden Gate and the Temple Mount, two sacred and important sites in His earthly mission. No wonder Jesus loved visiting this garden!

Golgotha

Golgotha, meaning "the Place of the Skull," is one of the two most common locations traditionally recognized as the site where Jesus Christ was crucified. While many associate Golgotha with the location now enclosed within the Church of the Holy Sepulchre, some scholars and Christian traditions identify another possible site near the Garden Tomb outside Jerusalem's Old City walls. This alternative location aligns with several biblical descriptions, offering a compelling argument for its authenticity as the place of the crucifixion.

This "Place of the Skull," discovered by General Gordon in the nineteenth century as a Protestant alternative to the Church of the Holy Sepulchre, lies near a rocky hill made out of limestone that has a distinct skull-like appearance. This feature, along with its proximity to an ancient tomb area, has led many to believe that this really could be the true site of Golgotha. Located just outside the Damascus Gate, this area was historically part of a major thoroughfare, also fitting the

Gospel accounts that Jesus was crucified in a public space where many could witness the event.

The debate over the true location of Golgotha continues to evoke passionate discussions among historians, theologians, archeologists, and pilgrims. Each site, whether the Garden Tomb or the Church of the Holy Sepulchre, carries profound spiritual significance. For many, the exact location matters less than the meaning of the events that unfolded there—the crucifixion and resurrection of Christ, central to Christian faith. Both sites serve as places of devotion, attracting millions of pilgrims from around the world.

Garden Tomb

The Garden tomb area, also called Gordon's Calvary, dates from the Roman or Byzantine period. In 1882, General Gordon identified it as the real tomb of Jesus Christ, although the location near the Damascus Gate is still debated by biblical scholars and archeologists. According to the New Testament, Golgotha, also known as "the place of the skull" in Aramaic, is mentioned as the spot where Jesus was crucified. Some theories suggest that the Garden Tomb perfectly aligns with this biblical description because it is so close to where Jesus would have been crucified.

The surrounding area, now maintained as a tranquil garden, provides a serene atmosphere for reflection and prayer. Unlike the Church of the Holy Sepulchre, which is steeped in centuries of ecclesiastical tradition, this location allows visitors to connect with the biblical narrative in a more natural and understated way. The simplicity of the site resonates deeply with those seeking an experience closer to how the events might have appeared in Jesus's time.

Archaeological findings near the Garden Tomb have added to the site's intrigue. The tomb itself, carved out of rock, aligns with the description in the Gospels of a new tomb owned by Joseph of Arimathea. While definitive evidence linking this location to Jesus's burial and resurrection remains elusive, its historical and geographical context supports the possibility that this area could, indeed, be the true Golgotha.

There is usually a long line to stand in if you want to have a moment to peek inside the garden tomb. The crowd is noticeably quiet and reflective here.

This outdoor garden area feels very different from the dark, crowded Church of the Holy Sepulchre. They both claim to be where Jesus was buried and resurrected. We just don't know the actual location, as there is evidence that proves and disproves both traditional sites. That's how it is in Jerusalem. Remember, it's not just about the place but the person: Jesus Christ. We don't have to see the exact spot to know that Jesus was resurrected and lives today.

When President Harold B. Lee visited the Garden Tomb in 1972, he said he was standing in a holy place and felt as if he could have witnessed the events that took place there. When President Gordon B. Hinckley visited the site in 2000, he stated, "Just outside the walls of Jerusalem, in this place *or somewhere nearby* was the tomb of Joseph Arimathea, where the body of the Lord was interred." The words "or somewhere nearby" were carefully included in his testimony because we simply don't know the exact location. We may never know with certainty until the Savior returns and points to the correct spot.

All Gospel accounts agree that a woman was the first to testify of the resurrected Jesus. Christ seemed to want to make a point of showing how important women are because a woman's testimony would never have been used in a court of law in Christ's day. All accounts also testify that we must tell everyone that Christ is risen.

The resurrection message consistent in all the Gospels is that

1. The tomb is empty.
2. We have all been rescued from physical and spiritual death.
3. Go and tell everyone!

The Birthplace of the Virgin Mary

Just inside the Lions' Gate in the Old City of Jerusalem, you will see an edifice with a sign that says, "Birth Place of Mary." It is maintained by the Greek Orthodox Church and is near the Church of St. Anne, Mary's mother. Someone is usually standing at the entrance and puts holy water from the Jordan River on your forehead with two strokes to symbolize the cross. There is a lot of artwork in frames, as well as murals that feature Mary as a queen. Candles light the space next to stained glass windows on the street level.

It looks quite modern, so be sure to walk down the two levels of steep, winding stone stairs to find small altars in the cave-like structure. It's hard to imagine all of that exists below when you're on the street level.

Like many Christian sites in Jerusalem, this location is not the only one that claims to be the birthplace of Jesus's mother, Mary. Another alternative is The Church of St. Anne in Jerusalem, while still another is in Nazareth. The Basilica of the Annunciation in Nazareth is very large and modern with several lovely courtyards. The church features an impressive collection of more than forty paintings and mosaics of Mary that were sent from countries all over the world. Her husband, Joseph, has the honor of a chapel upstairs named after him.

You may be wondering what the difference is between a church, cathedral, and basilica. It mostly has to do with Roman Catholic Church hierarchy. A basilica has been given special status by the pope for its historical, spiritual, or architectural significance. A cathedral is designated by the Vatican as a place of worship when it is the "seat" of a bishop or archbishop of a Catholic diocese. A church is simply a local chapel for a parish.

Church of St. Anne

This beautiful church is the best-preserved chapel built by the Crusaders just before AD 1140. The Crusaders found a simple cave on the site that had been built around AD 450 with a sign that was dedicated to "Mary, where she was born." The church is built above the cave.

It is set apart from the noisy, bustling streets of the Old City markets in the Muslim Quarter, right next to a peaceful garden courtyard, and just steps down, north of the Temple Mount. The Bible doesn't give us any details about where Mary was born, but the apocryphal Gospel of James, which is dated around AD 150, states that Mary's parents lived close to the temple, making this site credible.

The church marks the traditional site of Mary's parents, Anne and Joachim, Jesus's grandparents. Because of this, it is assumed that Mary was born and possibly raised here. The centuries saw the site in ruins and then later restored by the French as closely as possible to the original basilica.

It's a fantastic place to visit for a few reasons. It's just steps away from where biblical scholars and archeologists believe are the Pools of Bethesda, where Jesus healed a sick man (John 5:2–9). St. Anne's Church and the excavated compound of the Pools of Bethesda are currently maintained by the White Fathers, a Roman Catholic society of missionaries known for the white habit (tunic) that they wear. Nearby, there is also a museum and Greek Catholic (Melkite) seminary.

People also love to visit this church because of its incredible acoustics and reverberating echoes. Many choirs and church groups, including mine, go to the church just to sing a hymn.

I love that we get to see a beautiful sculpture of Mary with her mother. We don't usually think of Jesus Christ's grandmother, but surely, she had a powerful influence on the Savior. As a young grandmother myself, I think that we can serve the next generations with wisdom and love. We see a lovely sculpture of Anne teaching her daughter, Mary. It warms my heart to see the importance of education being passed down from a mother to a daughter.

In the church, we see portrayals of three seasons of Mary's life: the Annunciation, the Nativity, and the descent of Jesus from the cross. If you walk down a flight of stone steps, you will arrive in the crypt, a cave showing a simple altar to memorialize the original house of Anne and Joachim, as well as the suggested birthplace of the Virgin Mary.

The Western Wall

This is a true highlight of visiting the Old City of Jerusalem. At least it was for me. I had seen photos and videos of this site my whole life and

dreamed of going there someday. The energy and spirit I felt there did not disappoint. Plan your trip so you can attend Shabbat (Friday night) at the Western Wall. There is nothing else like it in the world. Be warned that it gets extremely crowded there on Shabbat, but being in the midst of that many enthusiastic worshippers is absolutely breathtaking.

The Western Wall, also known as the Wailing Wall, is just off of Ha-Kotel Street and is considered the most sacred site in all of Judaism. This portion of the giant wall is believed by all Jews to be the last remnant of the Second Temple, which was destroyed by the Romans in AD 70. The wall, measuring about 187 feet long in its visible section, is said to be part of the massive retaining wall built by King Herod during his expansion of the Temple Mount. For centuries, Jews have gathered there to pray, mourn the loss of their beloved temple, and place written prayers into the crevices of the ancient stones.

The Western Wall is a symbol of resilience and connection for Jewish people worldwide. Despite the destruction of the temple, the wall has remained a focal point of Jewish prayer and pilgrimage. It has

witnessed the turbulent history of Jerusalem and has become a unifying site for Jews who pilgrimage to the site. The plaza before the wall, created after the Six-Day War in 1967, serves as an open-air synagogue where people from all over the world gather every day for prayer, celebrations, and significant religious ceremonies.

You will see men wearing different types of worship clothing, depending on which Jewish sect they come from. I could write an entire chapter on just the fascinating and symbolic head coverings alone, ranging from hats, wigs, hairstyles, and scarves. The idea of covering one's head is a common practice among many religions and represents both a crown and a sign of respect and modesty to God. If you have been endowed in a Latter-day Saint temple, think of the head coverings and clothing worn there and what each piece symbolizes.

Ultra-Orthodox Jews will often wear a simple black velvet kippot (yarmulke) on their heads every day, which is a universally recognized head covering for Judaism. The practice of covering their heads is more a result of the various cultures than what is required by the Torah, the Jewish law.

Most of the men get pretty fancy at the Western Wall. My favorite is the shtreimel fur hat (usually made of mink or fox) worn by the married Haredi Jewish men on Shabbat. One of those gorgeous hats cost more than seven thousand dollars.

Jewish men wear a lot in their everyday worship too: a prayer robe, Phylactery, hats, and more. The images of their faithfulness are

absolutely stunning. Endowed members of the Church of Jesus Christ wear religious garments underneath their clothing. When I hear members of our church complain about wearing garments, I think of these valiant Jews and everything they wear to show God whose side they're on!

Before approaching the Western Wall, the Jews perform a ritual hand washing. Pay close attention to the many similarities there are to what Latter-day Saints do in our temples. The Jews often take a copy of the Torah with them to the wall to read passages while they rock in a rhythmic meditation. It's fascinating to watch the people get lost in their own worship.

Jewish women also wear head coverings and modest clothing. While they are not allowed to worship in the same area of the Western Wall as the men, they do not complain. Worshipping is a very personal, individual experience for them. A divider separates the men's and women's worship areas, each side offering chairs and complimentary copies of the Torah.

It is so touching to see so many Jewish women approach the wall with reverence to pray and read scriptures. On my first trip there, I noticed a young girl who kept looking around, searching for examples to follow and assurance that she was doing it "right." Eventually, she gained confidence and seemed to get lost in her worship, finding her own personal rocking groove. None of the women at the wall were asleep or bored; they were fully engaged in communing with God at this special place in the world.

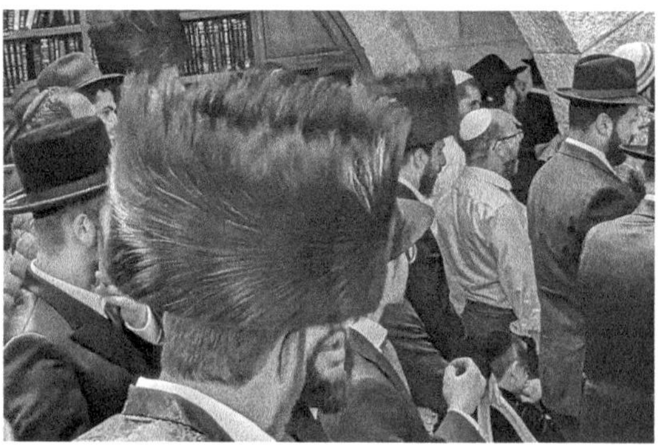

What really warmed my heart and brought tears to my eyes was seeing an older teenager who quickly approached the wall, completely prepared to pour her heart out to God. She placed her entire body against the giant stones and immediately began offering her sincere prayer with her arms and hands outstretched. She didn't hold anything back and didn't care what anyone thought of her worship. It was just her and God having an intimate conversation together. I want to be more like that! You can see her dressed in white in the photo above. In my mind's eye, I saw sisters of Israel as if they were at the veil in the Latter-day Saint temple.

At the Western Wall, Jews write letters and prayers to God on little bits of paper and then fold them into the cracks of the old stones. I had wanted to do that ever since I heard about it as a young child. I wrote my letter in advance and carried it with me to Jerusalem, so thrilled I would finally be able to add my written prayer to those of the faithful Jews in this land.

I had the immense pleasure of traveling to Israel with my twin sister on this special trip. Before we hid the secrets of our hearts inside the temple wall stones, she and I read our letters to each other and cried. Remembering that powerful moment brings tears to my eyes. There is such a palpable feeling of love for God in Jerusalem. It can change your life.

Every six months, a group of rabbis remove the papers from the Western Wall to make more room for new written prayers. Then,

they bury the sweet papers on the Mount of Olives. My prayer is now somewhere on the Mount of Olives to greet the Savior upon His return to this Holy Land!

Today, the Western Wall is not only a religious site but also a cultural and historical landmark. Adjacent archaeological excavations have uncovered additional sections of the wall and insights into Jerusalem's ancient past. The site is open to visitors of all faiths who come to experience its spiritual atmosphere and historical significance. The Western Wall continues to embody a profound sense of hope, faith, and the enduring connection between the Jewish people and their ancestral homeland.

After my sister and I experienced our quiet, sacred moments at the wall, a Jewish school from out of town brought their young teens who truly livened up the entire area. The crowds started to really pour in as the Sabbath evening approached. They sang religious songs, shouted, cheered, and gleefully ran to the Western Wall to join in prayer. It was breathtaking to behold. I wish our Latter-day Saint youth enjoyed the Sabbath day as much as this group of boys who were celebrating their Sabbath with so much joy. It was such a wonder and honor to behold and be a part of.

The BYU Jerusalem Center

I can't complete this book without mentioning the amazing BYU Jerusalem Center. It's lovely and has the most incredible view of the Old City. Visitors are invited to attend Sunday services in the breathtaking chapel, as well as wander around the grounds outside to snap photos of Jerusalem from the Mount of Olives.

The formal name of the center is the Jerusalem Center for Near Eastern Studies, but the Jewish and Muslim locals call it the "Mormon

University" or "Mormon Center." It is an academic campus of Brigham Young University, offering a fantastic study abroad program for students.

If you drew a line from its front door and circumnavigated that point across the globe to the United States, guess where it would end up? At the temple lot where the New Jerusalem will be built in Independence, Missouri. Coincidence? No. Amazing? Yes!

The two total solar eclipses that crossed over the United States in 2017 and 2024 literally drew an "X" on the continental map right over the New Jerusalem site too. Coincidence? No. Amazing? Yes! It was as if God were saying, "X marks the spot where big things are going to happen when Christ returns."

The scope of this book has not been about showing you all of the amazing sites in Jerusalem but to focus on the Via Dolorosa and the sites related to the last few hours of Jesus's life. I highly encourage you to add these fascinating locations to your list when you visit Jerusalem. Of course, there are also incredible places to visit outside the city all over the Holy Land.

If you can't visit Israel, consider watching videos on YouTube that teach you about these sites in the Old City:

- Cenacle (claims to be the site of the Last Supper)
- Church of All Nations (next to the Garden of Gethsemane)
- Church of Dominus Flevit (where Jesus wept)
- Church of Pater Noster (where Jesus taught the Lord's prayer)

- Church of St. John the Baptist (oldest intact church in Jerusalem)
- Church of St. Mark (claims to be the site of the Last Supper)
- Church of St. Mary Magdalene (Russian Orthodox church known for its seven gilded onion domes on top)
- Church of St. Peter in Gallicantu (its dungeon includes a cave cell where it is thought Jesus was detained for the night after His arrest)
- Church of the Ascension (its sixty-four-meter tower dominates the Mount of Olives skyline)
- Church of the Dormition (said to be the place where the Virgin Mary died)
- Church of the Redeemer (fantastic view of the city from its bell tower, ruins going back to Charlemagne)
- City of David (a fascinating archeological park)
- Kidron Valley (Jesus often walked here on His way to Bethany. It divides the Mount of Olives and Temple Mount. Fascinating funerary monuments.)
- Mount of Olives (Many events occurred here.)
- Pool of Siloam (where Jesus healed a blind man)
- Pools of Bethesda (where Jesus performed a miracle)
- Schindler's grave (to honor Oskar Schindler, who saved 1,098 Jews during the Holocaust)
- Shrine of the Book (modern structure shaped like a jar because it houses some of the Dead Sea Scrolls)
- Temple Mount (Al-Aqsa Mosque and Dome of the Rome are there but only Muslims can enter. It claims to be where the temple once stood. Your legs and arms must be covered when you visit the large space, but the Muslims provide temporary coverings for you at the entrance gate. Christians are not allowed to read the Bible there.)
- Tomb of King David (small Jewish chapel to honor the burial site of King David)
- Tomb of Mary (another site that claims to be the burial site of the Virgin Mary)
- Yad Vashem (Israel's official memorial to the Jewish victims of the Holocaust)

CHAPTER 18

Final Thoughts

Isn't Jerusalem amazing? What you have studied is only a brief introduction to the amazing sites in Jerusalem and the entire country of Israel. There is so much more to see and do. A common saying among Jews is "Next year in Jerusalem!" It's their aspiration toward an ideal return to their homeland. Many Jews go to Jerusalem three times a year to coincide with important harvest times: Passover, Shavuot, and Sukkot.

Jews who already live in Jerusalem say, "Next year in Jerusalem, the rebuilt!" referring to the building of the Third Temple, something they feel extremely passionate about. We know that the temple will be rebuilt and that the leaders and members of The Church of Jesus Christ of Latter-day Saints may play a special role in teaching the Jews about what happens inside temples.

The name of Jerusalem comes from two Hebrew words: "Yireh" (the Lord will provide) and "Shalem" (peace). Jerusalem was first called Salem in Genesis 14:18. Later, Abraham changed the name to Yireh (Genesis 22:14). Know God, Know Peace. No God, No Peace. As King David counseled us to do in one of his Psalms of Ascent, let us pray for the peace of Jerusalem (Psalm 122:1–9).

Another translation of the name of the city adds a layer of understanding and promise. "Jeru" in Hebrew means "you will see." "Shalem" in Hebrew means "whole." The name of Jerusalem is "Yerushalayim," which refers to a double portion, so the name of the city really means "You will see a double wholeness."

When we see how crazy the world has become, Christ's comforting words should ring loudly in our ears and hearts: "These things I have spoken unto you that, in me, ye might have peace. In the world ye shall have tribulation but be of good cheer; I have overcome the world!" (John 16:33) I added the exclamation mark because that sentence deserves it.

Being a disciple of Jesus Christ is not just one of many things we do. The Savior is the motivating power behind all that we do. He is not a rest stop in our journey. He is not a scenic byway or even a major landmark. He is "the way, the truth, and the life: no man cometh unto the Father, but by Jesus Christ" (John 14:6). That is the Way and our ultimate destination. The Via Dolorosa marks the way to finding Jesus Christ.

Robert Browning's poem "A Death in the Desert" describes what he imagined to be the death of John, the last of Christ's New Testament Apostles, who "saw with his eyes and handled with his hands that which was from the first, the Word of Life." Browning's poetic voice asks, "How will it be when none more saith 'I saw'?"

For roughly eighteen centuries, until the commencement of the Restoration in the spring of 1820, there were no prophets and no apostles. But then, suddenly, through the grace of God, there were eyewitnesses again, men and women who had seen with their eyes and handled with their hands. People who knew. The Church of Jesus Christ of Latter-day Saints truly restored the keys, doctrine, and gospel that

Jesus Christ established during His mission on earth. We are the only Christian church who doesn't just follow Christ—we are led by Him.

Jesus, the Resurrected Christ

The Via Dolorosa marks the path of sorrows, but it does not tell us the full story. Sorrow looks down. Worry looks all around. But hope looks up. Jesus didn't suffer only to pay the price of sin. He did it to help us change from our sinful nature and repent and be better, worthy, redeemed. Jesus doesn't just make up the difference when we sin; He *is* the difference. He doesn't fill up the gaps; it's about filling us with the love of God and the desire to be more like Him.

Station 14 of the Via Dolorosa focuses on where Jesus was buried. The absolute best part of this tomb is that it is empty (Luke 24:5–6). Jesus was resurrected and is alive today (Matthew 28:6).

In a 2004 *Ensign* magazine article called "Jesus, the Very Thought of Thee," Bishop Keith B. McMullin shared his sweet testimony in these words: "This Jesus, who is called Christ, wrought out a perfect atonement for all mankind by His incomparable life, His suffering in Gethsemane, the shedding of His blood, His death upon the cross, and His glorious Resurrection. He conquered the grave, and because of Him, so will we."

I felt that message deeply while in Jerusalem. We have been redeemed! We are saved!

The journey on the Via Dolorosa is not about the place but the person: Jesus Christ. Regardless of our struggles and sins, the invitation to come unto Christ extends to all. It's a message offering redemption to all who choose to accept it. In a world marked by uncertainty and turmoil, this principle stands as a beacon of light, reminding us that only in Christ can we find true deliverance, healing, and peace.

Jesus has risen! Even better, He's coming back soon!

ENDNOTES

1. Russell M. Nelson, "Peacemakers Needed," April 2023 general conference, Gospel Library.
2. "Summary Lesson 6: 'I Will Tell You In Your Mind and in Your Heart, By the Holy Ghost'," Israel Revealed, accessed March 10, 2025, https://www.israel-revealed.com/summary-lesson-6-i-will-tell-you-in-your-mind-and-in-your-heart-by-the-holy-ghost/.
3. 1958 general conference
4. Thomas S. Monson, "Ponder the Feet of Thy Path," October 2014 general conference, Gospel Library app.
5. Ibid
6. Bruce R. McConkie, *The Mortal Messiah: From Bethlehem to Calvary*, Volume 1 (Deseret Book, 1980), 18.
7. Pope Paul VI. *Nostra Aetate: Declaration on the Relation of the Church to Non-Christian Religions*. October, 28, 1965. https://www.vatican.va/archive/hist_councils/ii_vatican_council/documents/vat-ii_decl_19651028_nostra-aetate_en.html.
8. Neal A. Maxwell, "Overcome ... Even As I Also Overcame," Apr. 1987 general conference, Gospel Library.
9. Today, you can visit the Tower of David Museum, which features exhibits, tours, and cultural events that tell the story of Jerusalem's history over the past four thousand years. It is part of the Citadel, an archeological site with incredible views of the Old City and modern-day city of Jerusalem. You can go to the Lutheran Church of the Redeemer on Murstand Road to climb the bell tower for one of the best views of the Old City. On some nights, the Citadel hosts a fun sound and light show called "The Tower of David Night Spectacular" that tells the story of Jerusalem. You'll want to get your tickets to the light show online about three weeks in advance because they always sell out.
10. *The Jewish Encyclopedia: A Descriptive Record of the History, Religion, Literature, and Customs of the Jewish People from the Earliest Times to the Present Day*, Funk & Wagnalls, 1901–1906.
11. Conference Report, April 1927, 72–73.
12. C. S. Lewis, Mere Christianity (MacMillan, 1952).
13. Jeffrey R. Holland, "Lifted Up Upon the Cross," Oct. 2022 general conference, Gospel Library. Read Elder Holland's talk to learn more about how he answers the question about the cross. He even mentions the phrase "Via Dolorosa.
14. Teachings of the Presidents of the Church: Joseph Smith, 2007, 49.
15. Gordon B. Hinckley, "The Symbol of Christ," April 1975 general conference, Gospel Library.

16 Russell M. Nelson, "Integrity of the Heart," BYU devotional, Feb. 22, 1993.

17. Hal Leonard Corp., *CCM Magazine Presents 100 Greatest Songs in Christian Music* (Brentwood-Benson, 2007), 157.
18. Rudyard Kipling, *Puck of Pook's Hill* (London: Macmillan & Co., 1906).
19. Ulissess S. Soares, "In Awe of Christ and His Gospel," April 2022 general conference, Gospel Library.
20. Liberto de Caro et al., "X-ray Dating of a Turin Shroud's Linen Sample," *Heritage* 5, no. 2 (2022): 860–870, https://doi.org/10.3390/heritage5020047.
21. Jeffrey R. Holland, "Lifted Up Upon the Cross," October 2022 general conference, Gospel Library.
22. Ezra Taft Benson, "In His Steps," CES fireside, Feb. 8, 1987.
23. Jacob M. Braude, *Speaker's Encyclopedia of Stories, Quotations, and Anecdotes* (Prentice Hall, 1956).
24. Leo Buscaglia, *Living, Loving & Learning* (Slack Incorporated, 1982).
25. Brigham Young, *Journal of Discourses* (1859), 8, 345. https://www.churchofjesuschrist.org/study/manual/teachings-brigham-young/chapter-35.
26. J. L. Jones, J. L. (1973, June 12). "Big Rock Candy Mountains," *Deseret News*, June 12, 1973, https://www.theideadoor.com/other-pages/printables/other-printable-quotes/anyone-who-imagines-that-bliss-is-normal-quote/.
27. *War* 6, 449–451.
28. Jeffrey R. Holland, "Lifted Up Upon the Cross," October 2022 general conference, Gospel Library.
29. John Flavel, *The Method of Grace in Bringing Home the Eternal Redemption: Being the Second Part of Gospel Redemption* (1699).
30. Jeffrey R. Holland, "None Were with Him," April 2009 general conference, Gospel Library.
31. Lois Tverberg, Listening to the Language of the Bible (En-Gedi Resource Center, 2004).
32. Darrell L. Block and Ruth Judges, *The New American Commentary*, vol. 6 (B&H Publishing Group, 2003).
33. If you want to learn more about this scripture, visit Scriptures.byu.edu, which lists more than one hundred general conference talks about this scripture alone.
34. Max Lucado, quoted in "A Tale of Two Gardens," Bible Apologetics—A Daily Devotional, October 31, 2022, https://bibleapologetics.org/a-tale-of-two-gardens/
35. Lucian De Crescenzo *Il Caffè Sospeso: Saggezza Quotidiana in Piccoli Sorsi* (The Suspended Coffee: Daily Wisdom in Small Sips) (Mondadori, 2008).

About the Author

Dr. Trina Boice grew up in California and moved to Las Vegas a few years ago. In 2004 she was honored as the California Young Mother of the Year, an award that completely amuses her four sons.

She's a number-one best-selling author of thirty-five books, with another hitting store shelves soon. You can see them all on TrinaBoice.com. She coaches authors at FromBook2Business.com and has created quite a few online courses for professional and personal development at LifelongLearningEducation.com.

Trina currently teaches online for BYU–Idaho and is a volunteer service missionary, teaching institute in the Pathway program. She's also a film critic at MovieReviewMom.com. You can find her on YouTube as Movie Review Mom.

She graduated Summa cum laude with her doctoral degree in Management with a concentration in Higher Education Leadership.

Her master's degrees are in Healthcare Administration and Community Wellness Promotion. Trina earned two bachelor's degrees from BYU (Provo) where she competed on the speech and debate team and the ballroom dance team. She was president of the National Honor Society Phi Eta Sigma and served as ASBYU Secretary of Student Community Services.

Trina also studied at the University of Salamanca in Spain and later returned there to serve a Latter-day Saint mission in Madrid for eighteen months. She has a real estate license, travel agent license, and a black belt in tae kwon do, although she's the first one to admit she'd pass out from fright if she were ever really attacked by a bad guy.

She worked as a legislative assistant for a congressman in Washington, DC and was given the Points of Light Award and Presidential Volunteer Service Award for her domestic and international community service. She wrote a column called *The Boice Box* for a newspaper in Georgia, where she lived for fifteen years. She writes for several websites and is currently the Entertainment News Editor for BellaOnline.com.

Trina has gone on several speaking tours in China, Colombia, Mexico, and Puerto Rico. She loves to travel all over the world and now shares her travel tips and tricks with others at EmptyNestTravelHacker.com.

Trina was selected by KPBS in San Diego to be a political correspondent during an important presidential election. If she told you what she really did, she'd have to kill you.

If you enjoyed this book, please leave a positive review on Amazon or Goodreads. Thank you!

I would love to hear your feedback on how I could make this book even better. You can contact me at trinaboice@gmail.com.

More Books by Dr. Trina Boice

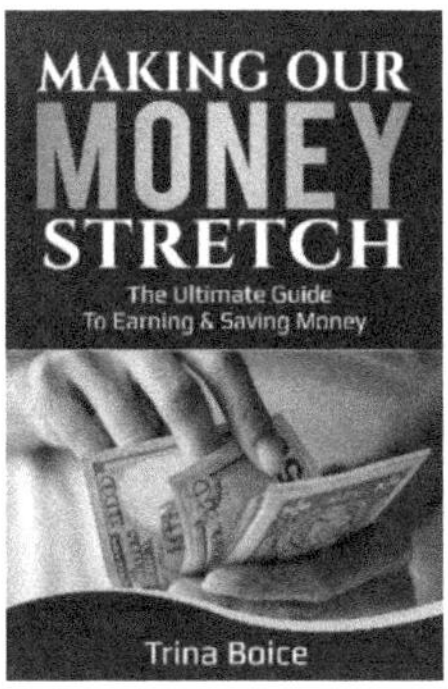

https://amzn.to/2DtxIKy

https://amzn.to/2PNW9bh

https://amzn.to/2ARSGjy

https://amzn.to/2QHBOFb

https://amzn.to/2WJ0XhV

https://amzn.to/2Dry6cl

https://amzn.to/2D8Pbqx

https://amzn.to/2JNkt7G

https://amzn.to/2qCgD8N

https://amzn.to/2Sg2o5l

https://amzn.to/2KHmBhD

https://amzn.to/2TRmHrk

https://amzn.to/3BcWCJp

https://amzn.to/35Sv54e

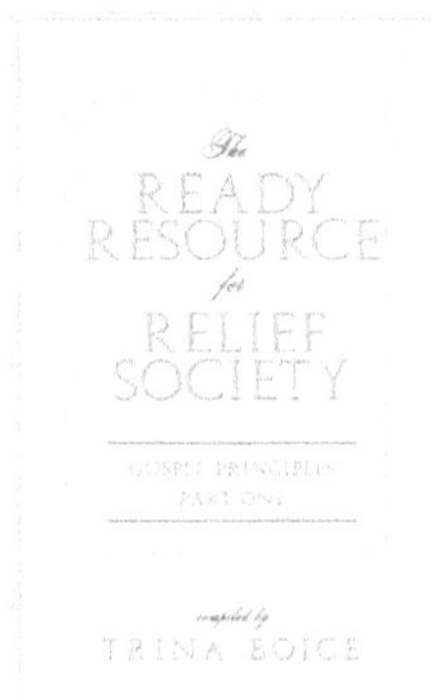

https://amzn.to/34oFiFu

https://amzn.to/2TUdRcn

https://amzn.to/2TTvgC1

https://amzn.to/2E0UY2T

https://amzn.to/2F9veTd

https://amzn.to/2FjIk0q

https://amzn.to/2DtbUii

https://amzn.to/40dYYo5